THE LIVE PAINTER™

Turning Your Art Into Income by Painting Weddings and Other Events

Lauryn Ahearn

www.thelivepainter.com

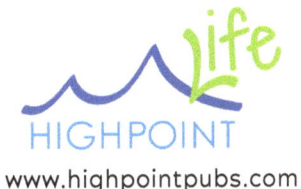

www.highpointpubs.com

This edition published by Highpoint Life Books
For information, write to info@highpointpubs.com.

First Edition

ISBN: 979-8-9862590-7-9

Library of Congress Cataloging-in-Publication Data

Ahearn
The Live Painter™
Turning Your Art into Income by Painting Weddings and Other Events

Summary: "This book provides everything any artist needs to know in order to experience the joy that comes with getting paid to paint—and attend a party while they are at it!" – Provided by publisher.

ISBN: 979-8-9862590-7-9 (Paperback)
1. Art 2. Business

Library of Congress Control Number: 2022923905

Cover and Interior Design by Sarah M. Clarehart

The Live Painter™ is pending trademark by Lauryn Ahearn LLC.

Manufactured in the United States of America

This book is dedicated

to my grandparents,

Irwin and Shirley Lazar,

who always supported me

in any dream I've pursued.

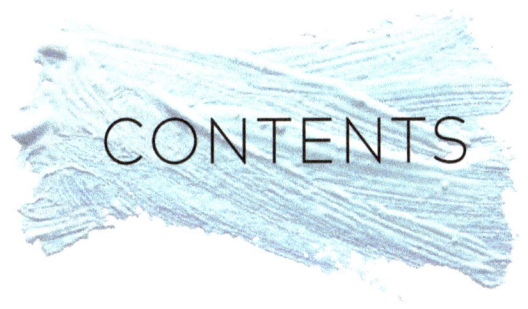

CONTENTS

ACKNOWLEDGMENTS

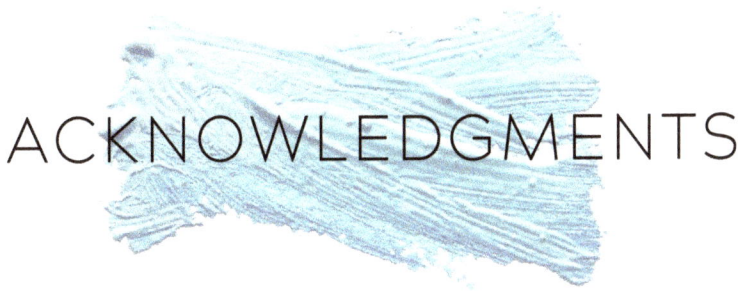

I'm very lucky that I have so many supportive people in my life who have helped me get to where I am today, and who have helped me as an artist, as a Live Painter, and in writing this book! First I want to thank my husband for his unwavering support in every way. No matter what dreams and schemes I come up with, you are always there to help me.

Thank you to my friend Amanda Bergman for getting me through so many events and always cheering me on. Thank you to my dad, Matthew Ahearn, for all of the business advice over the years. Thank you to all of my art teachers and professors from Mason Gross for developing me as an artist, and to Bonnie Diana for developing my foundation. Thank you to Frank May for giving me so many opportunities to exhibit my work.

Thank you to Michael Roney and Sarah Clarehart at Highpoint Executive Publishing for helping me put this book into the world! And finally, thank you to the clients who have hired me for your events and commissions (whose names I will omit for privacy). Each of you directly helped to make my dream come true by trusting me to paint for you, and I am truly grateful.

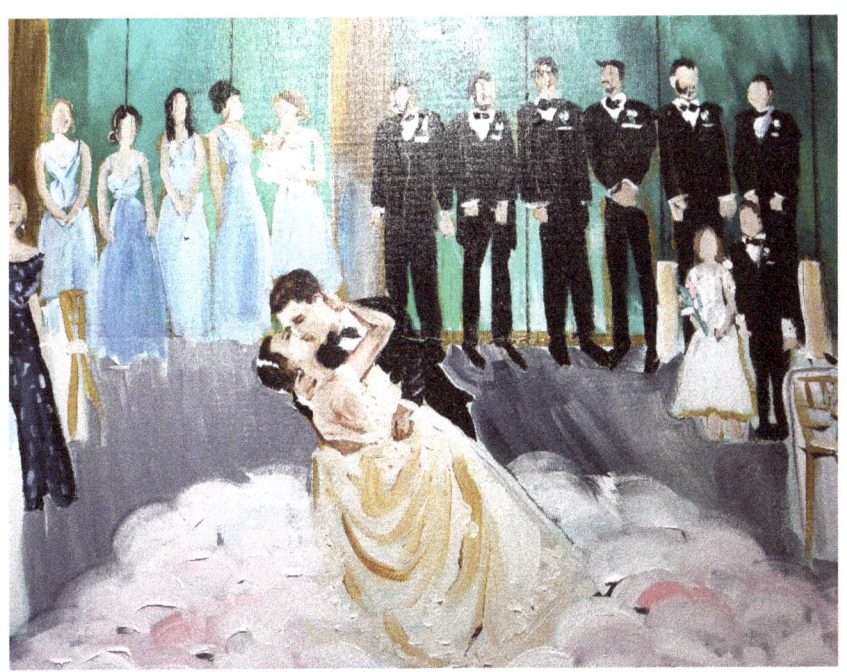

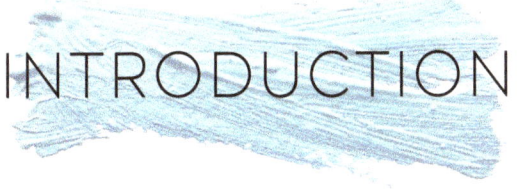

INTRODUCTION

People ask me all the time, how did I become a Live Painter™? I'm always struggling to answer this question in a succinct way, because the whole story is complex and spans almost my entire life. The thing is, I've always been heading in this direction.

I'm one of those people born as an artist. My earliest artistic memory finds me at about three years old. I was coloring on my parents' living room coffee table, and suddenly the limits of the paper felt too constricting. I needed to grow, to stretch. And so I colored all over my parents' table.

I'll never forget how hard it was to scrub off the marks (yes, even as a three-year-old, I had to clean it up).

That urge essentially sums up the relationship I had with art for the rest of my life. When I was a child, art was my safe place and my way to earn praise. Since I was naturally good at it, I felt drawn to it as the one thing that promised to bring me attention from my parents and my classmates. But please don't think I painted only for the feedback of others—that was just a bonus that spurred me on, a childhood incentive.

No, even as a child the real reward was the pleasure I received in rendering the visions in my mind before my eyes. The power to manifest the unseen, from the mind's eye into the physical world, is creator like. It is essentially an act of whatever god or energy you may believe in.

When I was six, I remember participating in a walk-a-thon at school. I was chatting with a classmate about our favorite subjects. Naturally mine was art. My classmate explained that she really did not like art class, which was shocking to me. "How could you not like art? Art is everything we see around us!" I didn't know it, but my art teacher was walking behind us at the time and overheard our conversation. She pulled me aside to tell me how right I was and how wonderful it was that I already knew this.

When I was a child, art was my safe place and my way of being seen. I would retreat to drawing on my own for thousands of hours when I was young. When I drew in class at school, kids would always ask me to show them how I drew things. They wanted to watch the process, because drawing something from a blank piece of paper is only one step away from magic. I was a mini Live Painter even then.

I drew and drew for years growing up, improving by taking occasional art lessons paid for by my grandparents and by poring over books that showed the process of Disney animation. I learned the proportions of the figure and how to create a body from shapes and expression with line. In high school, I was strongly influenced by my art teacher, Ms. Bonnie Diana. Ms. Diana loved art, and she loved her students' love for art. She had a beautiful heart, and the art room was a place where teens could talk about their troubles with an adult who would listen. It was a place where we could crank up music and be free. It was also where I would learn to transition from drawing to painting on an easel ahead of my grade level.

I was also a bit of a performer as a kid. It was another form of protected escape from a turbulent home. I could stand in front of people and be seen, but I would also hide behind my character. Starting as early as fifth grade I was cast in lead roles in school plays. In high school I was in the drama club and performed in community theater. As an impassioned teenager I initially wanted to study acting in college, but my parents forbade it. Oddly enough, they considered studying visual arts to be a more stable choice, and as much as I felt dramatically oppressed at the wizened age of sixteen, when I look back now, I'm glad things happened as they did. Life led me to study visual art at Mason Gross School of the Arts, the art conservatory at Rutgers University New Brunswick, and I know that was destiny. In an art conservatory program, some of the normally required liberal arts credits could be replaced by extra studio classes toward my degree. I developed my portfolio, my skills, and my understanding of realism and conceptual art in classical, modern, and postmodern history. I learned the foundational tools of art, and then I promptly learned to destroy them by pushing the boundaries of my own design.

I had a connection in the fashion industry. My grandfather had been the owner of a major company called Jones New York Coats, and so he helped me gain an internship in college working with the fashion designer of the company. This experience is how I landed my first few jobs after art school in the fashion industry, but I could quickly tell that this setting was not for me. The cutthroat and superficial nature of the fashion industry made me anxious, and I started to become ill.

I switched to teaching art. I worked toward my certificate to teach in New Jersey by working at schools for special needs students from underserved inner cities, but I quickly became depressed. The students needed so much more than what the school could provide. They needed food and adequate housing; they needed parents who were present for them. It broke my heart that I couldn't do more than an art project with them for forty-five minutes a week. This is where the healer in me began to take over and I returned to school again in my mid-twenties, but this time it was to become a registered nurse.

I felt a calling to learn how I could help people in a way I had never done before, which is why I made the ninety-degree switch from art to nursing. Most people don't realize there is a strong connection between medical science and visual art. One simple example is the dexterity and depth perception that a nurse needs to start an IV; it can be strengthened with life drawing practice. My interest in teaching others also served as a bridge between the two worlds for me.

Registered nursing was a noble day job, and it provided the living I needed to support my family, but I had difficulty finding a way to keep my art practice going in the first few years. I was exhausted from nursing home and hospital shifts. I didn't have the space I craved to paint freely. Before I knew it, I went and got married and had children of my own, which created a whole different kind of barrier to my art practice.

Looking back, I realize that any time I shied away from making art, I became depressed. I knew this during my second pregnancy, and I became determined to use my maternity leave not only to connect with my second son but also to reconnect with my artistic practice. I started painting again. I prefer canvas, but works on paper were more portable. I spent hours painting and drawing on the floor next to my baby boy, which helped me manage my postpartum depression and anxiety. I signed up as an artist on social media pages, and began to share what I was making with others consistently for the first time since art school.

In January 2018 my husband and I had an infant and a three-year-old, and my maternity leave had plunged us deeper into debt. I really needed some extra money, but the thought of picking up extra shifts at a hospital made me cringe. I had done caricatures at parties as a side job in art school by getting gigs from a party company, and thought it might be fun to open a business of my own doing this. Like many people, I had not yet even heard of live event painting.

One day, shortly after I launched my caricature business, I was scrolling through Instagram and I happened to see an artist I followed—someone who lived in the South—was painting weddings live.

I've had several distinct moments in my life where I saw someone do something and immediately said to myself, *I'm going to do that.* It's like love at first sight followed by stubborn and unrelenting determination.

Within two months I had transitioned my caricature business to live event painting, and it took off very quickly. I was making consistent money as an artist! It felt amazing to have the recognition and to be able to make a substantial side income for my family.

Painting live events combines both my love of art and performance, and I am able to sell artwork that is meaningful to my clients, while I have the satisfaction of knowing their paintings would be cherished family works of art for generations to come.

I have been honored to attend so many major life celebrations and capture those moments from my own point of view. If you've ever watched any of my vlogs on YouTube, you can see the joy on my face as I paint and perform. When people ask over the din of a crowd and thumping music how I become a Live Painter, I always pause for a moment, thinking of the long journey that brought me to standing in front of them. Then I look at them and say, "I've been an artist my whole life, and one day I decided to do this." And I smile because I know I have the satisfaction of working at one of the coolest jobs ever.

There was some concern among friends and family that by writing this book and "divulging the secrets" of the highly specialized live painting business arena, I would actually create my own competition that would push me out of the market. I feel that this kind of thinking is what keeps artists from banding together to form alliances and educate others about the value of original works of art and the importance of the creative process for everybody, not only the artistically inclined. Artists are frequently paid less and live below the poverty line. They are asked to compromise on their process and prices, and their contributions to society are overlooked. I've always been an educator at heart, and I feel the call to teach others how to make a living with their art. That's why I've written this book, and why I coach artists on live event painting. I want every artist to have the equal opportunity to experience the joy that comes with getting paid to paint—and attend a party while they are at it!

PART ONE:
You Can Be a
Live Painter

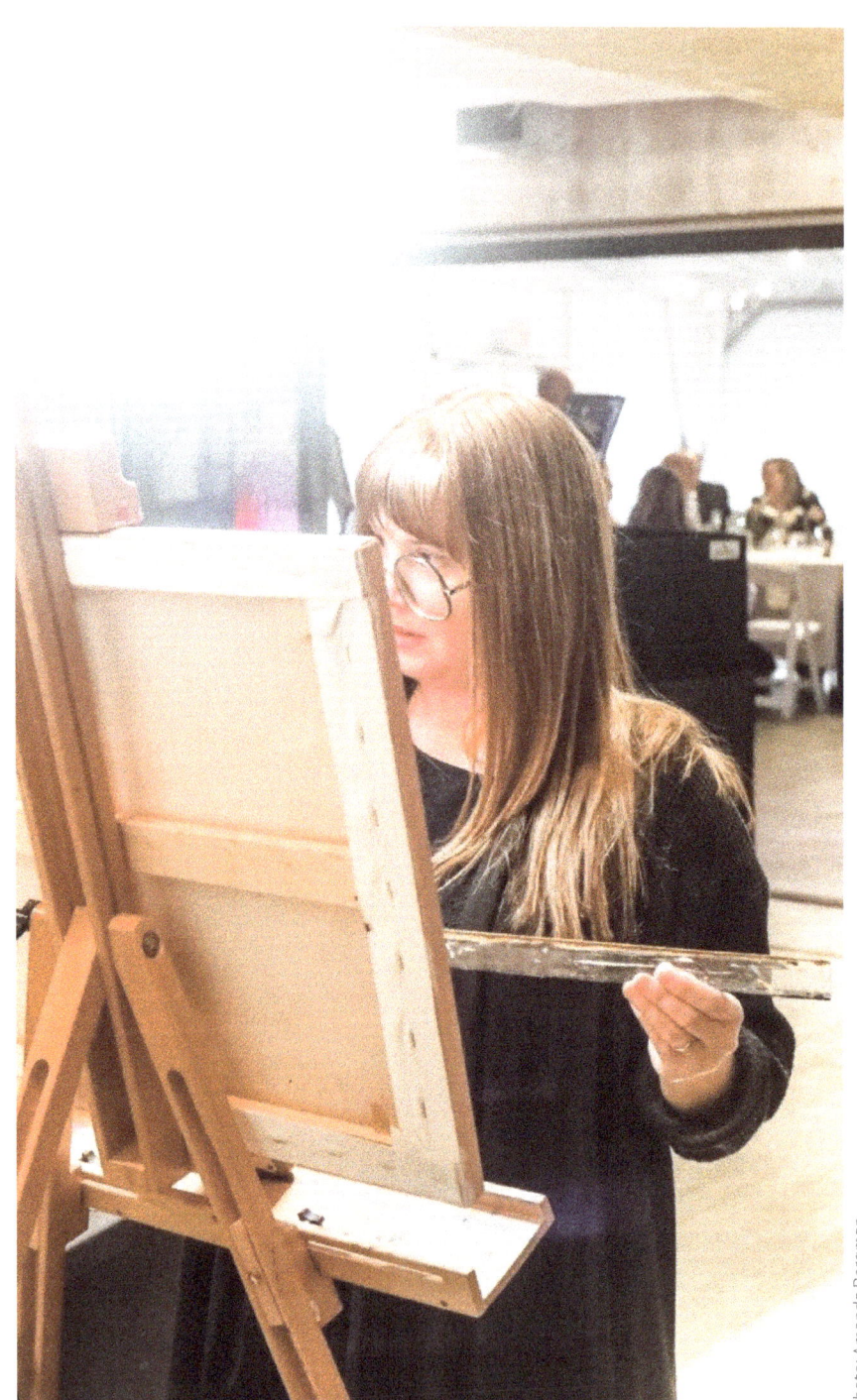

1

WHY LIVE PAINTING?

Why be a Live Painter? Live event painting is no doubt one of the coolest jobs ever for anyone that loves to paint. There is nothing else like it as an artist. If you are a painter, what is not to like about getting paid thousands of dollars in one night to do something creative and awe inspiring at a party?

It goes deeper than parties and money, though. As a live event painter, I am a witness to some of the most important moments in my clients' lives. I am blessed to be present for these moments, and on top of that, my artwork will be hanging in their home, which fills me with pride. With every live painting I complete, I have a work of art I made that others will look at every single day. These paintings will become cherished family heirlooms. Imagine what it would mean to you if you had a painting from your grandparents' or great-grandparents' wedding day that was passed down from generation to generation? To be a part of that family story, that lineage, is most definitely an honor.

Live event painting is also important because of the power in a painting itself.

When I was a senior in high school, our AP studio art class took a field trip to the Museum of Modern Art (MOMA). It was my first time there. I remember seeing Jackson Pollock's painting *Number 31*. I had learned about Pollock in class and was fascinated by the concept of abstract expressionism. I knew that the work of these artists was supposed to be a manifestation of post–World War II emotion that could not be otherwise communicated with the weight of how the world had been transformed by trauma. I had seen the famous films of Pollock's creative process, in which one can witness his mind transporting to another plane as he makes his brush movements. I remember staring up at the painting at the MOMA, inspecting it inch by inch and trying to feel the raw emotion Pollock felt when he made the original marks. It was as if the painting swallowed me whole—I was inside a world of mark making and emotion.

At that moment I did not know how deeply *Number 31* had affected me, but I would come to realize that it was the first time a work of art truly moved me, and ultimately that connection solidified my desire to work as a professional artist. Pollock himself could not have known the impact his artwork would have on a seventeen-year-old fifty years after he made it, and who knows how many others have had their lives touched or their paths altered simply because they laid eyes upon his work. The ripple effect can't be seen, but it is very present.

The Power of Art

What is the power of a work of art? In our technology-based world, some argue that painting is irrelevant. In my opinion, it's more important than ever. Modern painting is the manifestation of our earliest expressions as humans. Research says early human cave paintings were the first signs of true civilization, because it was the first activity that had no bearing on survival—it was entirely altruistic, created for the purpose of sharing with others.

Works of art primarily communicated visual stories and memories that had no other way of being documented—after all, there were no cameras and no way to take a selfie for most of humanity's existence. However, art remains much more than a picture of what the eye sees. It communicates important moments, creates windows into life experiences, and shares emotions that would otherwise be impossible to visualize. It brings us to a place where literal word and thought cannot venture.

The impact of a work of art on the person who sees it cannot be measured. Looking at a painting is like the moment a spell is cast upon you—your mind cannot unsee it, and the experience instantaneously transports you to a place you have never been before, whether that was intended or not. It cannot be controlled. If you even look at a work of art, it has an effect on you. There is no way to know the full impact of a work of art on anybody's life. Viewing a work of art is like the butterfly effect—the concept that a butterfly flapping its wings in one part of the world can be what creates a hurricane somewhere else. There is no way to trace the hurricane's cause to the flap of a butterfly wing, but that doesn't negate the contribution the butterfly had to the manifestation of the hurricane.

We may not be able to always pinpoint the impact viewing a work of art has on us, but it will impact us nonetheless.

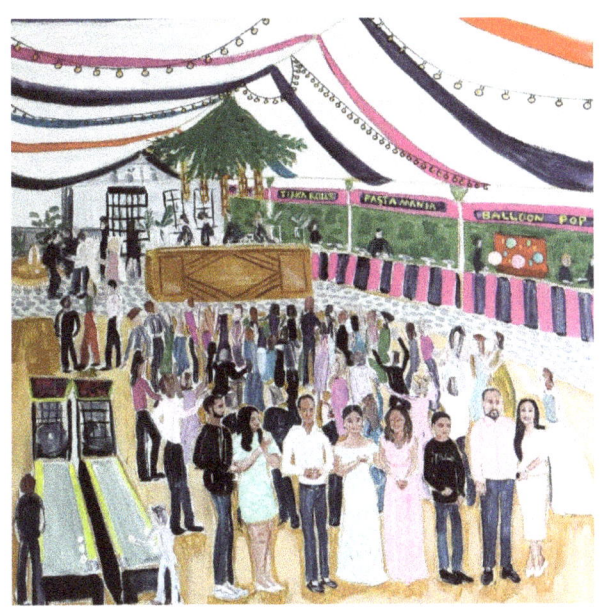

2

QUALIFICATIONS AND EXPERIENCE

You don't need to have live event painting experience to be a live event painter, but there some skills that really help and there is one *major* prerequisite: you have to know how to paint. This book will not teach you the fundamentals of art making and it will not teach you how to paint. I write this book from the assumption that you come to it with at least an intermediate level of artistic skill.

You're an Artist

Live event painting is an advanced level of painting skill. Not only do you have to know how to paint, but you have to be able to do it well and with an audience. Painting well doesn't mean painting like a photograph or painting compositions that look like weddings. Painting well does mean you need to have the foundational keys of color, composition, perspective, line, form, and value well under your command in whatever style you paint in.

How do you know what level of artist you are? Here are a few questions to help you determine your level:

- Have you ever received formal training?
- How long did you study?
- What kind of classes did you take?
- Have you ever shown your work in a gallery?
- Have you sold any art before (with formal training or not)?

The answers to these questions speak to your level of professional experience as an artist prior to becoming a live event painter. None of it is a requirement, but having some of these experiences means you are more likely to be an intermediate- to advanced-level artist.

If you've never had formal art training, you may not really be sure how good you are as a painter. It can be difficult to get an honest assessment of our own artistic skill. I offer portfolio reviews as a live painting coach, where I will give you honest feedback that you can use to assess where your skills currently stand and know what you need to improve. This is valuable information. It can be difficult to hear criticisms of our art, but professionals should deliver criticism constructively and enumerate specific things you can take away from the critique and target.

You're a Performer

Now, what about that little mention I made about needing to be able to paint in front of an audience as a Live Painter?

If you are stage- or camera-shy, I'm sure that caught your attention. Performance is the other part of live painting. It's live after all, which means eyes will be on you. Extensive experience painting in front of others is not a requirement at all, but you must prepare yourself. Before I started my live event painting business, I had a side gig as a professional caricaturist, and I was familiar with drawing pictures of people with a crowd of onlookers while under pressure because of a time limit. With live event painting, where you have hours to finish just one work of art, it feels a bit like a leisurely walk in the park compared to the intensity of caricaturing at large events when everyone is waiting in line for their own individual picture to keep.

If you've any experience with public speaking or performing, that's likely to help. While you aren't necessarily talking in front of a crowd when you live paint, you still are communicating with an audience. Being aware of your body, your expression, and how others will interpret that information while watching you get into a flow is part of what will keep the guests of the event—your audience—engaged in more than just the image on the canvas. You want them to feel the creative flow for themselves and experience the excitement that comes with the unpredictable magic of an unfolding work of art. Your audience is not only your subject; they are also conduits of energy. To witness the painting is to become a part of the soul of the work in progress.

Before I started to wax poetic, what I was saying was yeah, you *do* have to be able to stand up in front of a crowd of people without having a meltdown. And to be a painter who receives rave reviews and referrals, to be an artist at the top of the list, means that you need to make the process of painting an experience that guests can't stop talking about. If you aren't all the way there, that's okay. It's not as much of a prerequisite as having an intermediate to advanced level of painting skill is. I can't teach you how to avoid feeling the burning of eyes upon you, but I can teach you how to fake like you adore it!

You're a Businessperson

The third most important aspect of being a successful live event painter is more behind the scenes. It's about your experience in business. I really didn't have much entrepreneurial business experience when I started as the Live Painter, but thanks to my smaller business as a caricaturist, I was familiar with more of the business aspects of working as a live event painter than I would have been otherwise. I understood some basic marketing techniques; I already knew how to make a website that gets people's attention and how to use social media to get gigs. I had written and negotiated contracts for events. I had already been doing my own basic bookkeeping. And of course there are basic business skills, such as being able to communicate in writing, maintaining some control over your public image, and knowing how to use technology.

If you feel a little behind in the business aspect of being a professional artist, basic business courses are offered at local community colleges or by small business coaches online. There are also endless free resources for new entrepreneurs on the internet thanks to social media. As far as this book goes, I will give you some basic business lessons and more advanced business lessons that apply specifically to live painting.

What Is Your Voice?

The last thing that helps is having a voice as an artist, although it is not a requirement for starting as a live event painter.

An artist who has some level of professional experience and has been creating art for long enough has usually discovered their own voice in their work. Every artist has a unique style that is theirs alone, even if it is inspired by an artist or movement that already exists. There is only one way to uncover your unique voice as an artist, and that is to keep relentlessly making art. The more art you make, the more you fine-tune your own approach, color choices, flair, and brushstroke communication. The more you are aware of what your painting fingerprint looks like, the easier it is to be a Live Painter. And, if you already have your style defined, you are less likely to be influenced by what other live event painters are doing.

One of the most exciting things about live event paintings is that even if there are dozens of other artists who serve the same area you do (this can happen in more metropolitan markets), no one else will make art that has *your hand* in it, your *unique experience*—and that alone will help make your product effortlessly unique. There is no competition in live event painting—there are only different voices. Event hosts are not attracted to the same painting products. Your voice may be the one that suits them best.

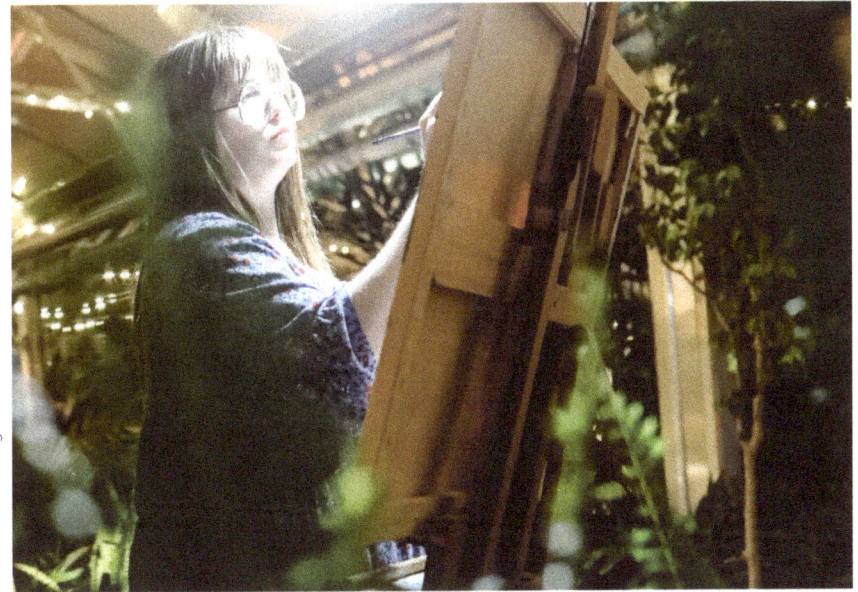

3

YOUR ARTISTIC FINGERPRINT

While most of this book talks about live event painting in the context of weddings, a wide range of events hire Live Painters: other private events, like anniversary or birthday parties, and corporate events, including team-building retreats, business expositions, conventions, and more.

While painting party scenes is the most popular subject matter for live event paintings, some artists specialize in abstract live painting performances. I've seen artists offer events where the guests leave input on a theme (for example, a business retreat wants a live painting on the theme of "teamwork"), and the painter creates an abstract or realistic work based on the input. Depending on what type of event and scene you are painting, your approach to executing your performance may need to vary. The information in this book applies to many different types of live paintings.

One of the most wonderful things about working in live event painting is that nobody can offer a product that is the same as yours. Your artwork is unique to you, like your signature and fingerprints. You do not need to try to have "a look" for your live event painting for this to be true—no matter what you paint, it will be painted by your own hand and therefore representative of your individual artistic flare.

There is a balancing act to having a "look," though, because while your work will always be in your signature style, there are ways to make that stand out among other artists, whether their style is similar to yours or not. Your style as a studio artist may be very personal to you, but a live event painter's artistic style becomes their brand. Your artwork is your own marketing in every way—colors, themes, composition. Every finished painting becomes a part of who you are as a Live Painter, not just as an artist.

It's a Catch-22. Your artwork will naturally represent your brand, but you have to make sure that brand makes a strong consistent statement, so you will find you do need to develop a sort of formula for all of your live painting work to create a reliable product. Another way to think of it is that having a consistent style for your live paintings helps potential clients know what to expect from you. Think about it—they are spending thousands of dollars for something that they don't even know if they'll like in the end. They are taking a gamble by hiring you, and if there is a sense of cohesion in your previous live event painting work, potential clients will feel more secure in hiring you for their event. They will feel that they have a sense of what the finished product will look like and will trust you to deliver something that fits what they pictured for their end result.

Remember that most people do not have an understanding of the artistic process unless they themselves are also artists. A potential client may have a hard time understanding how you can promise to give them a finished product they will love, because they don't know how to express their vision in words. However, if the client finds that they are drawn to each of your paintings in your portfolio again and again, they will feel confident in having you paint for them.

What are some of the styles of live painting you can choose from? This is partly determined by the medium and size you paint in. If you are more of a photorealist, you will likely be drawn to painting in oils, as there is a level of depth in color that is difficult to achieve with other types of paints. Or if you are a watercolorist, you may find yourself painting more ceremonies than receptions, as watercolors tend to be portable and are able to be finished relatively quickly.

Perhaps you paint in a very large format. You may prefer to work in acrylics instead of oil for cost savings. If you are an abstract impressionist and need thick texture for your works, a small watercolor approach would not be right for you.

If you are concerned that your art is not consistent enough to represent the style or brand that you have in mind for yourself, the best way to hone in on a developed style is practice. Practice painting and make samples again and again and again until you can see a thread of consistency throughout the works. If you cannot see it, potential clients also will not be able to see it, and they will be less likely to hire you.

Your performance style will also become part of your brand once you begin to accumulate events. Some artists are the silent type. They are quiet and choose to represent a sort of preconceived notion of the emotional and withdrawn artist, passionately painting in the corner of the room, deep in concentration.

Some artists emphasize the performance aspect of live event painting. For them, this process is more important than the end result. These types of live event painters are sometimes referred to as "speed painters." They perform large, high-impact artwork, often of celebrity images, in an overstated dramatic process such as jumping and dancing while painting, or painting entirely in splatter brush strokes.

Some artists are more glam—they perform as high-fashion, model-like artists, painting daintily, mingling with guests, and creating Instagram-worthy photo ops.

My performance brand is in harmony with the quality of my work—warm and sunny, colorful, and friendly. I am playful in both my paint application and my interactions with guests. I dance and bob to music as I work, and I smile constantly. Guests feel good watching me work, seeing my painting progress, and finally taking in the finished product. I happily answer questions and make sure I am always polite to everyone I meet, from the parking attendants to the waitstaff to the guest(s) of honor.

The best way to convey your performance brand is by offering videos of live events you have done on your website and social media. This is a little harder to develop as a part of your portfolio prior to your official launch as a live event painter. One way you can increase your video library is by starting out with charity events. I will provide more detail on this later in the book.

No matter what your performance and artistic styles are, the ability to paint swiftly and spontaneously under pressure is paramount. Even if you are an oil artist who brings works back to your studio after the event to work on them for two months, you will need to get enough visual information down on your canvas by the end of the night that guests can see at least some semblance of the finished product. It is also difficult to plan compositions for live events ahead of time, so when you first start painting at an event, you need to make quick decisions about things like the color of the underpainting, which you suspect may change when that beach sunset ends, or where you will paint the bride's and groom's parents in relation to who is from which side of the family.

You also cannot allow yourself to become nervous while people watch you work—you will lose precious time you need to get your work done. You must be able to tune out all of the distractions of the room if necessary—the changing dance floor lights, the din of the crowd, the blaring music, and the flashes of cameras. This does take some practice if you've never performed in front of an audience or have trouble with things like public speaking.

When I'm feeling nervous and distracted at a live event, I find that everything fades away if I force myself to solely focus on the artistic process. It's not easy, and it takes practice, but no matter how shy you are, I am sure you will be able to overcome any nerves once you practice at some events.

One of the things that will take the pressure off the first few times you perform is if you are charging very little to nothing for your performance and painting. When there is no pressure to please a client because they are already receiving the value of free entertainment, you are able to learn how to turn down the distractions so you can focus on your art. Eventually it becomes second nature, and you will be confident that you can get the job done to the expectations your client has of you.

PART TWO:

Setting Up Your Business

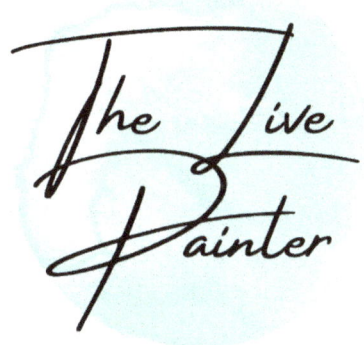

4

BRANDING YOURSELF

Business branding is a broad topic, but I have had experience in successfully branding myself as a Live Painter. Branding is essentially your identity as a business. In the age of social media, it can be a little exhausting to have to stay "on brand" with every public post. Still, you can build your brand, your *professional identity,* by projecting a consistent message about who you are and what you are about. That will help you establish your business as *the* go-to for live painting in your area of expertise, location, or style.

Everything you put out to the public reflects your brand: the look and feel of your website, every post you make on social media, every blog post, every photo, font choices, graphics, and colors. According to Lean-Labs.com, the five pillars of brand identity include:

1. **Visual brand identity:** When you're an artist, your visual brand identity is huge. This goes beyond your style of live painting, but your live painting style will be the biggest part of your visual brand identity. This is yet another reason why it's important to establish a style as a live event painter—it determines the story you tell customers about who you are.

2. **Brand voice:** Speaking of the story you tell: your brand voice is how you tell it. If you were going to make a commercial for your audience, what would the narrator sound like? Would they be excited? Soft and lilting? Loud and bold? Tailor your voice to your audience. For example, wedding clients are often looking for a romantic brand, while a painter who specializes in expos may be using a more fun, upbeat brand voice to attract event and party planners.

3. **Brand values:** What is important to you as a business owner? As an artist? Elegance and integrity? A commitment to fun? Be consistent in expressing these values to your potential and current customers.

4. **Brand personality:** If your business had a personality, what would it be? This will go right along with your visual brand identity as an artist. Remember that color plays a huge role in conveying brand personality as an artist.

5. **Brand message:** This is what you want your customers to know about you. A brand message is often simplified into a tag line or catchy phrase. For example, this book's brand message is "Get Paid to Paint while You Party."

Writing a business plan is not a prerequisite to starting a business as a Live Painter, but one of the areas business plans explore is branding. Writing up a business plan can help you answer some of those crucial questions about what messages you want to project before you get started. (See the business plan section in the next chapter.) It is much easier to establish your brand from the get-go than to launch and later try to walk back your look or messages, so don't be in a rush to make these decisions.

There are also plenty of free journal-type activities online to help you determine what your brand should be. Even the social media website Pinterest is full of blog posts by business experts that describe various methods of brand development.

Here are some fun and easy branding journal exercises that I personally found helpful and enjoyable:

- Write out your values for your business.
- Write out the personality traits of your business
- What colors could you use that would represent your values or personality traits?
- Is there any imagery that comes to mind that could represent your message?
- Pretend your brand is a celebrity. Who would it be? Why?
- Who do you know, in real life or fiction (from a movie, book, or TV show), who could represent your brand?

Who is Your Ideal Client?

Ask yourself this very important question: Who is your audience – your *ideal* client? You must know and understand the identity of your ideal client so that you can craft a brand story that speaks to them specifically. I don't just mean who would like your paintings. Rather, the question is who would be *obsessed* with them? Who really needs your services? Who would hire you over and over again? What is that person looking for? Where do they hang out? What are they interested in? How old are they? Where do they live?

A live event painter's ideal client usually boils down into two categories: wedding clients and corporate clients. However, there is a much deeper tunnel to follow from this point when profiling your ideal client. Let's say you are a wedding painter. Then, of course, your ideal client is a couple getting married. But what kind of wedding is your ideal client throwing? What is their budget? What are some common traits to weddings that would hire you as a live event painter? Where does your ideal client live? Are they a young couple? Are they having a traditional or religious ceremony? Are they a same-sex couple? Maybe they are having a destination wedding, and you can offer special travel packages as a Live Painter. Maybe your ideal wedding client isn't a couple at all, but the parents of the couple.

For corporate clients, you need to know if your client is hosting an expo, team-building exercise, product release party, or some other type of event. Maybe certain industries have more of your ideal client than others. Who represents and makes decisions for events for your ideal corporate client? You may want to connect with party planners, marketing departments, or human resources professionals, depending on the answers.

Here are some more fun journal questions to try to nail down your ideal client's persona:

- If your ideal client was a celebrity, who would it be?
- If they were a music genre, band, or song, what would it be?
- What would your ideal client's ideal event look like?
- What is your ideal client's biggest problem? How does your business solve that problem?

What's Your Elevator Pitch?

An elevator pitch is an important aspect of your business plan and acts as the mini version of your brand story. The concept of an elevator pitch is that it is what you would say to someone you meet in an elevator to get them intrigued about you and your business in the short time it takes to reach their floor.

Write down your elevator pitch, memorize it, and practice delivering it so that when your chance to share it comes up, you won't hesitate to clearly introduce your business to someone.

To figure out your elevator pitch, ask yourself: What issue are you solving? What is the solution you are selling to solve that issue? Who is your audience? What makes your solution special? Find a way to combine all of this information into two or three sentences.

What's Your Ideal Business Name?

Choosing your business name is a major step in establishing your public identity as a live event painter. This could mean choosing your actual name (for example, Lauryn Ahearn), choosing a formal business name (The Live Painter), or both. Many artists work their name into their business name—for example, Wedding Paintings by Joseph. Whatever you decide, there are a few things you should check off your list before you settle on your live painting name.

Is it original? You want your Live Painter name to stand out from the crowd. Do some online searching and find out the names of other live event painters both in your area and nationally. You do not want your name to be too similar to someone else's both for intellectual property reasons and for the practical reason that you do not want your business to be confused with another's. This is why combining your own name into the business name is a popular choice. There may be a few "wedding painters" or live painting business names that are already out there, but who else is going to already have the name Jennifer Smith Live Painting?

You cannot choose a name that is too similar to one already used by someone else, because you could be infringing on their rights. They can come at you with a cease-and-desist letter. I unfortunately learned this lesson the hard way with a previous business. I thought that just because I added a few words to the end of a business name it was different enough from someone else's. Then one day I opened my mailbox and I learned that this was not the case. The lawyer coming after me explained that the name was similar enough that potential customers were getting confused. My own lawyer said I didn't have a case, and so I had to give up the name and start over *after* I had already begun to build my brand, paid for my domain name, logo, and so on.

You will want to check and make sure your name is not trademarked by anyone. In the Unites States you can do this by going to USPTO.gov to check that your chosen name is not partially or fully trademarked by someone else.

Is it available? You'll also want to make sure the domain name is available. While a variation on your business name for the domain name may be okay, you don't want it to be too different from your business name, or it could confuse potential customers.

If someone has a domain you want for your website, but they don't have a trademark on the name, you may think you can lay claim to the business name, but beware: simply by owning a domain name an individual has some legal claim to the name even if it's not trademarked. This gets a little messy, so if you have any questions at all about this, you should speak to a lawyer who specializes in small businesses.

Another lesson I learned is to be careful about looking up your potential business domains. It's no secret that the apps on our phones, the cookies in our browser, and maybe even our microphones are always watching what we are typing and speaking about. I've looked up domain names that were available, thought about them for a day or two, and then gone back to them only to find out the name had since been purchased. Coincidence or conspiracy theory? To avoid this, make sure you have a handwritten list of your business name/domain name ideas before you start searching for availability, and be ready to make your decision fairly quickly after you look them up.

Is it memorable? Similar to making sure the name is not too much like an existing business or too complicated for the domain, you want to make sure the name is memorable. Easy spelling is also helpful, so if you have a long, difficult-to-pronounce last name, you may not want to use it in the name of your business. "The Live Painter" was simple and easy to remember, but I know my last name "Ahearn" is not easy to pronounce or spell correctly.

What does it say about me? This last question really ties into exploring your brand as a live event painter. With anything regarding the identity of your business, you want to ask yourself what it says about you. What is your persona as an artist and performer, which we talked about previously? For me, I felt "The Live Painter" made a strong statement that set me aside from other people who do live painting. It identifies me as *the* authority on live painting, it's simple and easy to remember, it tells people exactly who I am and what I do in three words, and it was happily available at the time I made my decision.

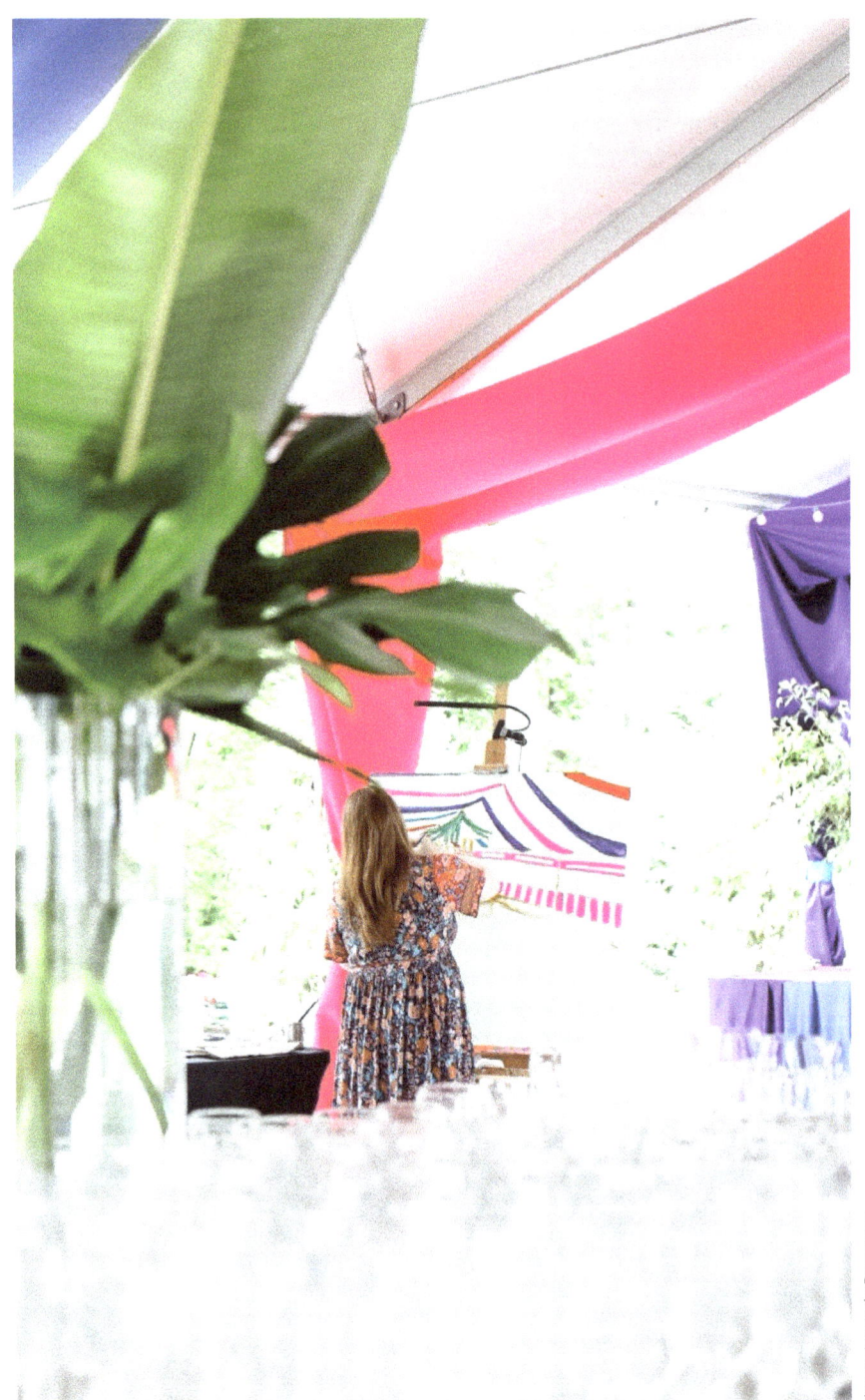

Photo: Amanda Bergman

5

THE BUSINESS TECHNICALITIES

Little business details like money and trademarking are not "fun" for artists, but if you want to grow your business, you have to face them.

Writing a Business Plan

A business plan will help you lay out the nitty gritty of how you plan to function before you launch. Because most Live Painters are individuals without employees, this simplifies the nature of your business. You may not even need to form an official corporation (most commonly for small businesses, this will be a limited liability corporation, or LLC). It is best to discuss your options with a small business lawyer and/or accountant who can help you determine what kind of business setup is right for you. Creating a business plan will help you determine your start-up budget, research the competition, and analyze your strengths and weaknesses. The internet is full of free business plan templates. Even the most basic ones will adapt easily to the live painting business model.

You should have a separate bank account for business transactions. Besides keeping your business funds easily identifiable for the government, having a separate bank account will also help you avoid spending client deposits before you actually paint the event.

You also need to track your income and expenses. There are many apps that make tracking cash flow, budgeting, and filing taxes easy. I personally enjoy using Hurdlr for my expenses because it is simple and mobile friendly. I figure if I can't categorize income and expenses on the go, then it's unlikely that I'll ever remember to do it!

I have included samples of several business documents in the book's appendix.

Setting Your Budget

When you start putting together your business plan as a Live Painter, you need to determine the different variables that go into pricing. You will likely have two different budgets—a startup cost budget and an annual budget.

Startup cost budgets include one-time expenses you need to launch your business, like hiring a business lawyer to incorporate your company, easels, and art supplies for initial samples. Looking at sample business plans can be very helpful with this, because they usually include a section on startup costs, and that will give you guidance for researching your estimates.

Your annual budget will include things like annual website domain registration and hosting fees, email fees, event website subscriptions, and ongoing supplies. Creating a budget for art supplies when you first begin can create an extra layer of challenges because you may not really know how fast you will burn through things like paint or brushes. An annual budget for art supplies will also entirely depend on how many events you book—the more events you book, the more supplies you will need. However, annual fixed costs are spread out over the total number of events. Because of this your cost per event will change depending on how good business is.

Here is an example of what I mean. Let's say your annual cost for websites, subscriptions, and other fixed costs is $2,000, and your supply cost for each event is an average of $200.

If you book four weddings, your per-event fixed cost is $500 ($2,000 divided by four events). Your cost of doing business for one event will be $700 ($500 + $200).

However, if you book ten events, your per-event fixed cost is $200 ($2,000 divided by ten events). Your cost of doing business for each event will be $400 ($200 + $200), which is almost half of the per-event cost if you only booked four events in a year.

As much as you may enjoy painting, you are doing this because you want to earn money, so you are going to want to charge for more than supplies.

Calculating Your Valuable Time

Time is another factor to consider when pricing your services. Time is not only the time you spend painting at the event. You must also consider things like prep time, travel time, and time spent finishing the painting in your studio if that's part of your process. There are also the many hours you will spend working on your business for no client in particular. This includes all of the time you spend updating your website, posting to social media, responding to inquiries, consulting with customers, and drafting contracts. When pricing anything hand-made, it's sometimes recommended to pay yourself an amount per hour you spend working on a project. I do not calculate my prices this way, but I still consider time as a factor, especially when I compare my rates to other Live Painters (more on that in a moment).

Some artists charge separately for their hours in the studio after the event, and some include it in their package pricing. It all depends how you want to set up your packages (more about that soon too).

Time spent traveling is not the only component of travel costs. You need to consider the price of gas, food, and hotel if it's an overnight, and perhaps a flight if you will be traveling a long distance. Some artists charge a flat rate for travel over a certain number of miles. I prefer to customize travel prices so that a client is not paying more or less for travel than they need to.

You can include your travel fees in the price you present to potential customers, or you can break out the travel fee. I've both included the travel fee in the prices I offer and broken the travel fee out, depending on the situation.

Shipping Costs

Speaking of travel, your painting may also need transporting! If you are not finishing the painting at the event, or you offer clients the opportunity for you to bring it back to your studio for touch-ups, you need to think about the cost of transporting it to your workplace and then back to the customer. Whenever possible I prefer delivering the painting in person. Your finished painting is truly precious, and you do not want to deal with the headache of your art being damaged in transit to a customer. If personal delivery is not an option, I highly recommend looking into a private courier who can deliver for you. You can use a commercial shipping company, too. However you choose to deliver it, you will need to carefully pack the painting to ensure there is no damage from bending, dropping, or moisture. Saatchi Art online has some excellent video tutorials showing how to package a painting to prevent damage. You can have the shipping company pack your painting, but that costs extra.

You also always need to insure your painting for no less than the amount you sold it for if you are using a courier or commercial mail delivery service, which is an extra cost to consider when deciding on how to price your work.

Taxes

Then, of course, there's everybody's favorite expenditure: taxes. When you get that beautiful payment for a painting, it's easy to forget that Uncle Sam is waiting for his cut. Whether you are filing your art sales as part of your personal taxes or as a business, you will need to remember that a chunk of your profit will be flying away. Make sure to set aside at least some of every payment for taxes, and check with an accountant to calculate the amount that's right for you.

So What Are Your Prices?

Optimally pricing your live paintings is a process that may take you some trial and error. Particularly in the beginning of your business, you will find yourself adjusting your pricing as you learn more about your specific business.

When determining your pricing, you need to consider many different factors, including:

- Cost of supplies
- Cost of business
- Time involved
- Travel
- Taxes
- Shipping and delivery
- Market rates/ competition

After you've been doing events for a little while, you should revisit your pricing. Event vendors tend to raise prices annually to keep up with inflation and market rates, and to reflect their experience and expertise.

Some Live Painters have beautiful PDF documents with all of their prices and packages laid out, so that when an inquiry comes in they simply send the potential customer the document.

All of this information is well and good, but at what price point do live event paintings really sell? The problem with this question is there is no single answer. I've seen live event paintings priced for as little as $600 to over $10,000. That's a huge spectrum, so it's hard to know where to start, but the best way to figure it out, besides calculating costs, time, and the other areas I mentioned is by researching the market near you. While there are not a lot of live event painters and there may not be one in your geographic area, you should research pricing of your competition based on similarity in size and style.

Here's an example of what I mean. One artist I know who charges $10,000 for some of their paintings works in a similar size range as I do, but I don't charge anywhere near that amount. This artist paints in a hyper-realistic style with oil paints, and while they paint at the event, most of the work is done after—they put in over four hundred hours of studio time. I, on the other hand paint in an abstract impressionistic style in acrylic paint, and I rarely take my paintings back to the studio. My approach is expressive and expansive. I would not dream of charging so much for a painting that takes me four to seven hours in a less expensive medium than the photorealistic oil painter.

Some live event painters are very forthcoming with their pricing and have it available on their website, while others will only give the information directly to clients making inquiries. You may want to research the competition. Just remember that event painting is a small circle, and we often refer one another when we aren't available for a certain event date or inquiry. You want to stay amicable and professional with other Live Painters. Remember, you can learn a lot from them too!

When I think of how to price my work, I always think of something I learned in a wedding photography course that spoke about how to price wedding photography: most clients do not really know what the price "should be" for your product. They will believe your art is worth whatever price you put on it. They will have a budget they are looking to spend, and they will look for vendors who are within their range. That means that if you sell a wedding painting for $2,000, you will appeal to some people looking to spend $1,500–2,500. But other clients may be looking to spend $3,000–5,000, and by having only a $2,000 package, you are missing out on potential sales because you priced too low. Ultimately, price as high as you can but where you are still making sales.

Pricing Packages

When a Live Painter creates a package, think of it more as a product. Your package is what you will offer your client, from nuts to bolts. Some painters include different extras at different price levels. Most of my packages differ only in the size of the canvas, but what is (or isn't included) remains the same across all packages. For example, some Live Painters include only a certain number of recognizable people in their packages. You'll notice several of the package aspects below are also on the list of what you need to take into consideration when setting your pricing:

- Travel
- Framing
- Number of recognizable people in the painting
- Size of the painting
- Hours spent on the painting
- Shipping/delivery

I offer six packages in a range of sizes that I have tweaked over the years. The price is incremental as the size of the canvas gets bigger. I usually include travel and a free display easel, as well as varnishing if it comes back to my studio. If the couple wants the finished painting shipped to them, I identify how much extra that would cost in the contract.

Negotiating Pricing

Once you do all of your budgeting and research, you will come up with your perfect packages, feeling confident at the price point you've arrived at, only to have potential customers try to knock the price down. Artists are generally insulted when people undercut the price of their work, but try not to take it personally—I've learned that haggling over price is common in the event industry. That doesn't mean, however, that you are expected to lower your price or negotiate. Because live event painters are a "luxury" addition to an event, don't be afraid to remain firm in your pricing. I have learned that those who cringe at the price tag don't truly have an appreciation for art and the work I do, and they are less likely to be satisfied with the final result. The best customers are the ones who see your value and are excited to commission a piece. Don't let too many low-ballers make you decrease your package pricing. This can be tempting, especially in the beginning, when you are desperate to get gigs. It's better to increase your prices over time than to drop them when your price point isn't working out. Doing your market research and knowing what your comparative competition charges will help you feel more confident about standing firm when someone asks you to cut them a break.

Here's something I learned the hard way: always include prices in emails so you don't forget the offer you made to a client. Sometimes customers come back to you weeks or months after you gave them a price quote, and you won't be able to remember what you offered them if you've been adjusting your prices since. Of course, if it's been a really long time, I wouldn't be afraid to bump the prices accordingly to your current going rate. To avoid this situation consider including an expiration date on your quote.

Special Packages and Partnerships

The coronavirus pandemic changed the way events will be coordinated forever. Because of the issues related to space and social distancing, clients and vendors were all forced to be more creative in terms of what they could make an event look like. For example, micro weddings became a popular option for those getting married during the crisis. Developing special packages for potential clients is like offering an exclusive product. One way to present a standout product is to partner with other vendors to create all-inclusive wedding packages. This can be a little challenging for Live Painters because our product is a luxury, and sometimes the price point simply does not work with a package wedding deal. However, there are other ways to come up with creative packages for your target audience. Your imagination and entrepreneurial spirit are your only limits.

Styled shoots are another great way to collaborate with vendors. A styled shoot is essentially a staged event, with models and product samples from all different types of vendors usually being arranged by a planner. You don't get paid, but you do usually get amazing free photos of yourself that you can use on your website and social media. Make sure to check with your planner about any restrictions on photo and video use from the styled shoot. Sometimes there are time limits on when you can share info because the shoot will be published in a magazine or blog.

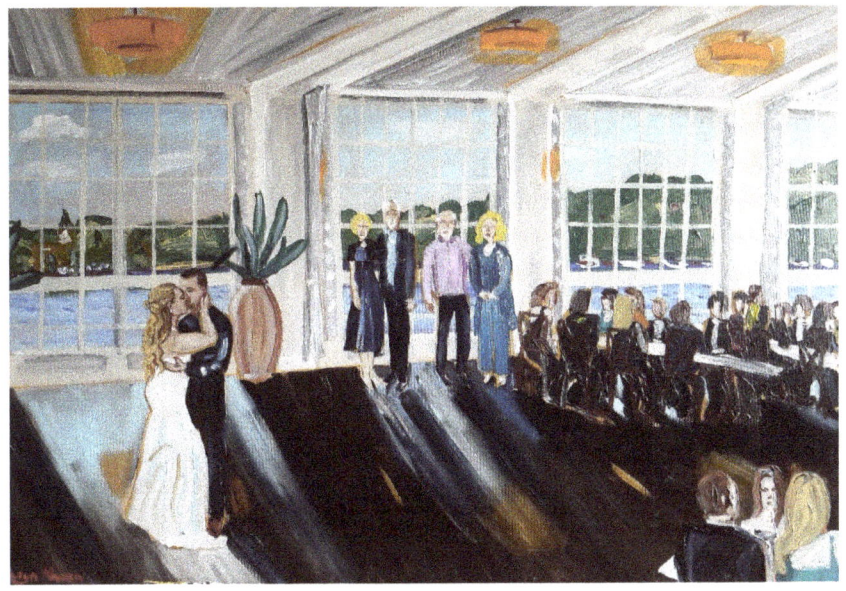

6

BUILDING YOUR WEBSITE AND VISUAL BRAND

Your website and extended visual brand are hands-down the most important business tools at your disposal. These days, most people will not consider hiring anyone who does not have a website unless it is someone they personally know. Your website is the visual and written manifesto of your business. It is your mission statement and your brand statement. It is where you will make a first impression on many of your clients. It should be both informative and enjoyable to visit. If it's not all of these things, then you are losing out on a major opportunity.

Every aspect of your site, from design to photos to the tone of the web copy, needs to unify the message you want to project to others as a live artist. Because nailing every detail on your website is so crucial to your business, hiring a professional web designer will be the best possible investment you could make to grow your business. A professional knows just what content you need on your website and often can provide customized graphics for you as well. A professional also knows how to design your website while maximizing the power of your search engine optimization (SEO). SEO is what determines how high up the internet search engine list you appear when a potential client types something like "Live Painter" or "live wedding painter near me." I have had more business from effective SEO than I have from bridal expos and bridal websites combined.

If you aren't ready to take the plunge on hiring a web designer when you are starting out (especially when you are doing samples and free charity gigs), there are some amazing affordable website hosting sites that can make professional looking sites for you (Wix.com is my personal favorite. It provides scores of professional templates that allow you to create and update a professional-looking site, and then requires that you pay an annual hosting fee to them.)

If you are making your own website, you will need to decide what to include and how to organize it. Do some research by checking out other Live Painter websites to see what information they include. You can even look at mine! Check http://thelivepainter.com to see firsthand how I set up my site.

My website content includes the following:
- An introduction to my business
- Information about myself and my experience as an artist and live event painter
- An explanation of how live event painting works
- Frequently asked question and answers

- A gallery of my live wedding paintings
- A shop with my artwork for sale
- Testimonials
- Links to my booking form
- Contact information and social media links
- Video blog (vlog) episodes of my live paintings
- Commission information
- My blog

The story of your business should also be told in all graphics and images on your site. Your logo is the first visual aspect of your business you need to consider outside of your artwork. Websites are usually designed around the colors and feel of a company's logo. Many painters are also handy at graphic design, so if you feel up to the task, go for it! There are also free apps like Canva that enable you to easily create your own logo, display signage, business cards, website graphics, and more.

The downside to using these types of free services is that the templates are not always the most original. For a completely customized logo, signage, and so on that is as unique as your artwork, hiring a graphic designer may be another startup cost you would want to budget for.

Building Your Portfolio

A portfolio of your live paintings—composed of samples that convey your brand and style of work—is critical to your selling your service through your website. You will need at least a few samples on your website. Of course, this is a chicken-and-egg thing. You haven't yet completed any paying gigs, but nonetheless you need to produce some paintings. You can begin by painting a few friends and family events. You also can work from photos of other weddings. Just be careful to choose photos you have permission to copy for this purpose; otherwise, you may get in trouble for copyright infringement. Do not paint from photos of famous or well-known scenes and then try to represent that they are your own, or sell them for money. Not only will it leave you open to legal trouble, but if people browsing your work recognize the

41

image is from somewhere else, your reputation will take a big hit. You also don't want to lie about your samples being painted from photos, but you don't need to make it blatantly obvious either. Your credibility as a live event painter is as good as your clients perceive it to be. It's okay to create the illusion of experience as long as you are ready to deliver the authentic thing when someone hires you for pay.

Your samples need to tell a prospective client what they can expect from your live product. Keep in mind the difference in quality and finishing touches between a painting completed in the studio and one completed live. You do not want to make your samples perfect photo replicas unless that is what your live paintings will also look like. When I paint samples, I try to paint in about the same amount of time I would have for a live painting so that it doesn't look too highly veneered or overworked. There is a spontaneity and a loose hand seen in live paintings that is born from their being genuinely painted live. I try not to linger too long over certain details the way I might normally in the studio. Try not to let your sample paintings be too perfect.

I am frequently asked by new Live Painters how many samples they should have. I would say the number is less important than the representation available. You want to have at least one painting in every common scene you plan to paint and in different canvas sizes, as this will change the level of detail you incorporate in a limited-time setting. For example, if you plan to paint weddings, make sure you have indoor and outdoor ceremony paintings and indoor *and* outdoor reception paintings. I would recommend no less than six samples to start with, but the more images you have of previous work, the easier it will be for you to nail your first full-paying gigs.

Photos

A graphic designer may be able to edit photos for your website, but unless they are also a professional photographer, you will likely need to get the photos yourself. Quality photos on your website are crucial to attracting clients. You don't just need photos of your art. You need photos of yourself in action. Don't skip hiring a professional photographer for your website photos. They turn the level of professionalism you will project way up. When looking for a photographer who can capture your art performance essence, look at photographers who specialize in the same types of events you do. If you are a wedding painter, then hire a wedding photographer to do your shoot—an on-trend photographer will be able to take attractive photos of you optimized for the latest eye-catching bridal style.

Videos

Your videos on your website are also crucial to nailing down gigs. I have two types of videos on my website—the first is a professionally filmed and edited video of myself while live painting a styled shoot. This is the video on my main page at the time of writing this. It acts as a commercial, as it were, to anyone visiting my site.

The second type of videos I have on my website are VLOGs of live painting events. These videos are not as polished as my styled shoot video because they are composed of rough footage I took myself with a tripod while I work the event, or they are video shots filmed by my assistant on her phone. Then I have a professional VLOG editor remix my footage into something palatable that tells the story of the event and shows my potential customer what it's really like to see me in action. (Yet again I am making sure they understand what my product is so that there is no disappointment or miscommunication over the end result).

Styled shoots are a great way to get an amazing package of photo and video at a discount. In the wedding industry, a styled shoot is when a number of wedding vendors get together to create a mock wedding, so that everyone has something to walk away with for their website, portfolio, and other marketing. The first styled shoot I attended was organized by a wedding planner and included bridal wear vendors, florists, bakers, stationers, photographers, videographers, and of course the wedding venue itself. I was an extra for the styled shoot, which would be submitted to different wedding blogs by the planner. I received free professional photos by an amazing wedding photographer of myself at work while I was fully dolled up for the camera. The wedding planner was working with a videographer on compiling footage for her own marketing video, and since the videographers were going to be filming me anyway, I asked if we could strike a deal: they used their footage to make a video for me to use as well (I checked with the planner organizing the whole event to make sure she was okay with this). The video was a little pricey, but it was worth the investment for a perfectly filmed live wedding performance.

Other Aspects of Your Visual Brand

Your visual brand extends beyond your website and even your artwork to the space you paint in. Your Live Painter setup should fit with the story you are trying to portray, down to the type of easel you use. Your painting space is your "stage," and you need to set the scene accordingly. Signage serves two purposes: it helps set your stage, literally and figuratively, and it conveys important information in a simple way to your audience.

Over the years, my signage for live events has transformed as I've homed in on what works and what doesn't and as my budget has increased. I keep a little painted sign with my @thelivepainter social media handle by my easel, so that when people take pictures I can gesture to the sign and suggest they tag me. I also have a sign more akin to an advertisement that includes my name, website, and information advertising my previous live television appearance. You may need to make signage for practical purposes too, depending on what you need your audience to know—for example, requests to stay out of the artist's space, or encouragement (or discouragement if you don't like free publicity) to take photos and videos. Remember to keep your signage in your performance space consistent with the branding on your website. Use the same font and colors. If you used a graphic designer, get a quote to have them make your signs too.

Your visual brand extends to your business cards as well. There are lots of free resources online to make business cards, but if you have a graphic designer make sure to have this included in your design package. There's nothing more refreshing than a seamless visual story that carries across all of your marketing materials. Make sure to have plenty of business cards with you at every event. I keep them somewhere that guests can easily reach since I usually have paint all over my hands. When I am cleaning up at the end of the event and my easel and painting are the last things left, I always put some business cards on my easel. I leave my signage up until the last minute as well because a lot of audience traffic occurs at the end of the event, when guests check in to see the end result of your night's work before they leave. This is when you will get your biggest reactions as people marvel at the progress you made over the course of the event.

Social Media

Besides word-of-mouth referrals and strong SEO for your website, social media will be your biggest way of attracting potential customers. There are different strategies for posting on social media depending on the platform you are using (Facebook, Instagram, TikTok, LinkedIn, or whatever else is "in" at the time you are reading this). But the first strategy is to pick your platforms! In order to pick the right platform to actively invest your time in, you need to know where your ideal client hangs out online. In my experience, parents of couples getting married hang out on Facebook, couples hang out on all of the social media sites, and event coordinators and planners can be best connected with on LinkedIn. Instagram is a great crowd pleaser for every demographic because it completely revolves around visual posting, which has the greatest potential impact for you as a visual artist. When posting to social media, do some research on when the best time of day and day of the week is to post. Each platform is different. And no matter which platform you are posting on, the most important element is consistency. Posting consistently—at least once a day—will draw the biggest following possible and encourage active engagement on your posts, which usually brings you more viewers because of the way social media algorithms work.

Promoting Your Brand Elsewhere on the Internet

Your online presence goes beyond your website and social media and extends into event websites. Bridal websites like The Knot and Wedding Wire and party sites like the Bash are all popular ways to attract customers. Some of these websites allow free listings, and some do not. Some offer a very basic free listing and you have to pay a monthly fee for a more detailed profile or higher ranking in search results. It may or may not be worth it for you to pay for one of these sites. To help you decide, calculate how much a yearly subscription would cost and how many events you would need to book on that website at your rates to make a profit. For example, I need to book only one wedding on TheKnot.com to profit from the subscription, which is an easily attainable goal for me.

Online reviews on these websites as well as Google are also extremely important. Encourage previous clients to leave reviews on the site they booked you through in order to boost your visibility and credibility. I always wait a little before I follow up with a customer after an event, especially if it's a wedding, because I know the clients are decompressing from their milestone.

Remember, whether you are talking about your social media profiles or event site profiles, your brand should extend to every place your business exists on the internet. Consistent visual storytelling creates a polished, professional look and helps your clients know what to expect.

When you receive an inquiry through a website, social media, email, or phone, do not delay in responding. Statistically speaking, the early bird gets the worm. Clients often contact several vendors at once to compare services. The sooner you respond, the more likely they are to book with you. It's helpful to develop a response template so that when people reach out to you, you can quickly copy and paste your reply. Just be careful to customize the reply before you send it! It does not look professional to accidentally answer with someone else's name or event date (I know because I am totally guilty of this). Also, always include all of your contact information in your response. Even if someone emailed you first, put your email in your signature at the bottom. You want to make it as easy as possible for potential customers to reach out when they are deciding whether they should book you.

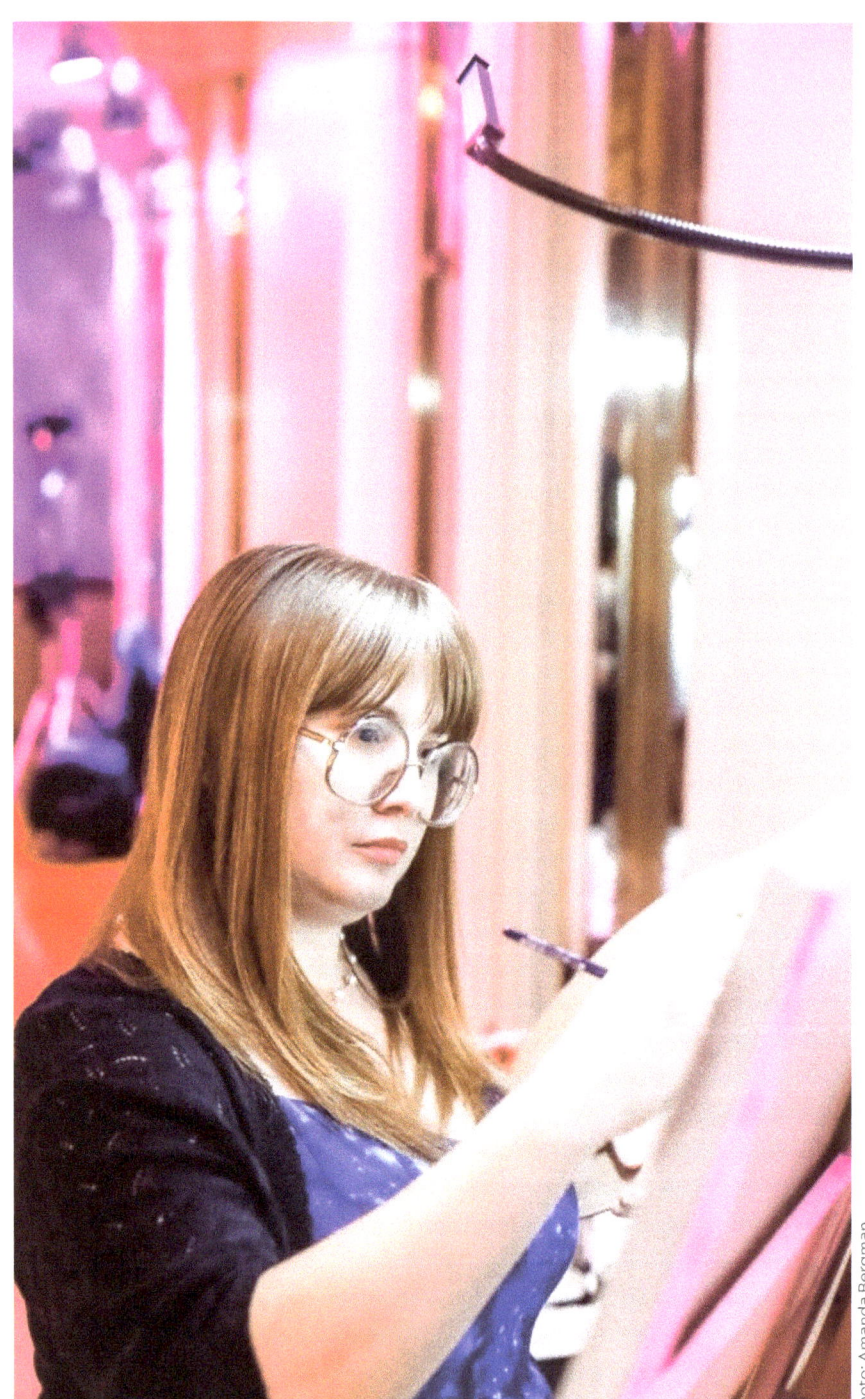

7

GETTING YOUR
FIRST GIG

Getting your first position in any field is usually a Catch-22—a tough situation for which the only solution is one that is not actually possible under the current conditions of the problem you're trying to solve. For example, you need experience to get the job, but you need the job to get experience. Live event painting can be a Catch-22 like that: in a regular day job, you might break into an industry by interning for little or no pay. You have to start with live event painting the same way. But before we get into live gigs, let's talk about practice.

Unless you regularly paint party scenes for fun or money already, you will likely need some practice at painting these types of gatherings without the pressure of painting live. In the comfort of your studio, you can apply different techniques, rework new ideas, and time yourself for events. You also need to build up a portfolio, and practicing from photos is the best way to develop one when you've never done a live gig. You don't need to advertise that these paintings were done for practice when you share them on your website and social media—nobody needs to know (unless they specifically ask you). Practicing will also help you hone your style and your brand, which is crucial to success as a live event painter.

Once you have a systematic approach to painting your samples in your studio, you are ready for your first live gig. Just like an intern, you will want to find someone to paint for and charge them little to nothing. I always tried to negotiate for a basic supply cost when I first started.

Painting for Friends and Charity

Painting for friends or for charity is the best entrance option. Some people stumble into live event painting because they are an artist and a friend asks if they could paint their wedding. Other people work spontaneous live events at bars and festivals. My first live event painting was a birthday party for one-year-old boy whose mother had a malignant brain tumor. Her friend was putting together a large party at her house for the occasion so that the mother could have a memorable birthday with her son and none of the stress. I was so moved by the gesture that I volunteered to do a live event painting for only the cost of the canvas. Of course that was an amazing way to commemorate such an important family moment, and they were eager to have me paint the party. I had very little pressure on me since I was doing the work for free. (And that's a good thing too—that painting was definitely not up to the standards I would require if I were going to charge more.) It also helped me work out some of the unexpected logistics of painting at a party on site, like juggling gear with transportation, loading, and unloading.

I graduated from painting small charitable events for free to larger charitable events that included auctions. In some ways those larger events are preferable because you may be able to negotiate a base amount with the entity holding the event in order to offset your costs. The safest approach for you would be that the auctioneer agrees to pay a minimal fee for the painting if it doesn't sell, or you set the minimum bid at a price you are comfortable with. You paint the event, and the auction occurs a little prior to the end. Whoever wins the auction and purchases the painting gets their likeness painted in.

Finding opportunities to participate in an auction is not too difficult. You can start by cold contacting an organization that has an annual fundraiser, ball, or other event and offer your services to see if they are interested in striking a deal. The organizations often jump at the chance, as long as auctioning the art fits the event vibe or their mission as an organization. Because art auctions are usually considered a classy affair, this is not often a problem. With auctioning live paintings at events you have all the benefits of live practice and exposure with less risk if the painting's end result fails to please the crowd (spoiler alert: it won't fail). You also have more opportunities to network with venues and future clients attending the party.

Ultimately, networking and referrals are the most effective ways to get work in any industry, and the event industry is no exclusion. No matter what type of live event you specialize in or market to, if other people are buzzing about you, you are more likely to get work. Since you are starting off with free live paintings for friends or charity, you are building your portfolio and exposing your work and process to everyone who sees you. With your branding on point and your painting and performance skills honed, guests who see you will not easily forget you. At least 75 percent of the people I encounter at events have never seen or heard of a live event painter. This puts me at advantage because now when they do think of live event painting, I will be the quintessential artist they think of. And since my business name is easy to remember, they won't have a hard time steering curious friends in the right direction. And there *will* be curious friends, because the people who see you paint live at an event will be so enthralled, so captivated, that they are going to tell everyone they know who is planning a wedding or large party how they saw a Live Painter at so-and-so's wedding, and how amazing it was. Before you know it, you will have a strong portfolio and experience that give you confidence and lead to your first full-paying client.

Other Ways of Getting Gigs

If you are planning on focusing your business on conventions and corporate events, you may be able to find a talent agent to represent you. Finding an agent can be tricky because live event painting is a newer and unique branch of the entertainment industry, so you won't be able to just look up agents who specialize in it the way a singer, comedian, or model is able to. I recommend looking for agents who specialize in the event type you want, not necessarily organizing your search by vendor representation type. You may find an agency that offers a lot of variety or specialty acts or specializes in business events that would love to add you to their roster.

Becoming a preferred vendor at venues is another way to reach potential clients. Most venues have some sort of preferred vendor list they give to their clients, with recommendations for everything: music, flowers, photography, and more. Being on a preferred vendor list means a venue is telling their clients that they can be connected with other businesses that can be trusted to do their job well. Many venues will not list more than two or three recommendations per vendor type, and they may turn inquiring vendors away because they already have a table linens company they usually work with. Since you are a niche entertainer, you don't need to worry as much about competing with other Live Painters for a preferred vendor listing at a venue, and venue coordinators are often enthusiastic about adding a new type of entertainment to their list.

PART THREE:

At The Event

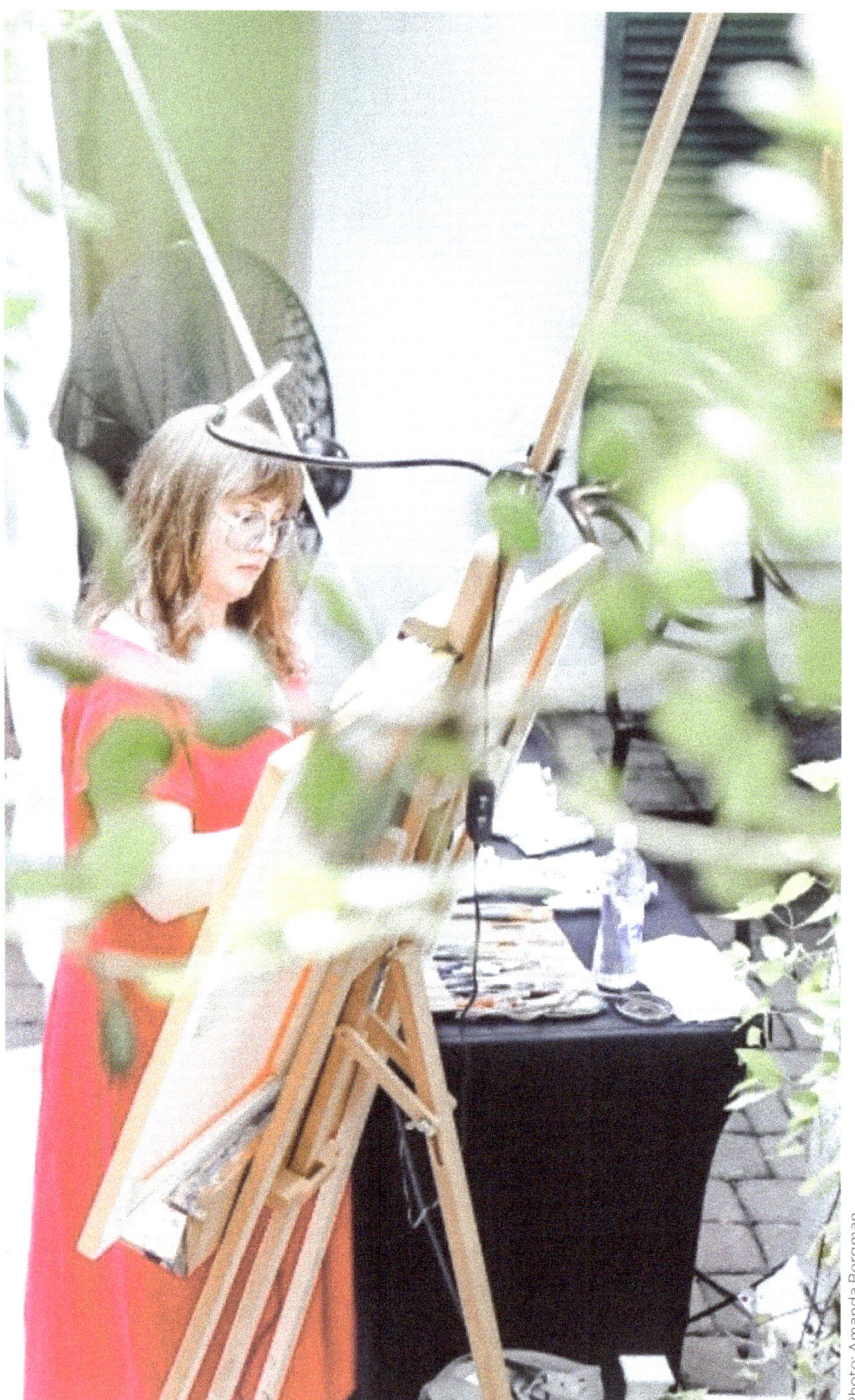

8

SETTING UP

You've got your first gig. Congratulations! Now, take a deep breath and don't panic.

After you've booked this momentous occasion, I recommend that you first think about how you will get to the event. First, *always* add extra travel time when calculating your estimated time of arrival. You *do not* want to be late to a wedding, and you don't want to be in a rush either, especially if you need to start painting prior to the event. Let's face it, you can always kill an extra half hour painting more details or mingling with guests, but you can't get that time back if you arrive late.

When you get to the venue, tell the parking attendant that you are a vendor and need to unload. The staff will tell you where to enter and if you need to park somewhere other than where the guests park. Some venues have loading areas specifically for vendors, usually by the kitchens, while others will have you enter through the front.

It's sometimes a long trek from the car into the room or area where you will be painting, so don't carry anything too heavy on your first walk in. I like to grab my canvas first, because it's reasonably light and the most delicate cargo I have. It also signals "I'm the Live Painter" to anyone I meet who doesn't know what my role is. I've been yelled at by staff for entering a reception hall before it's open to guests because I dress more like a guest than a vendor. (I have learned from my work as a vendor that it really would be easy to crash a wedding. As long as you don't sit anywhere for dinner, anybody dressed nicely and walking with purpose can walk into a wedding reception…not that I would recommend doing that!)

Finding the Best Painting Location

Your location is one of the most important things to consider for your entire painting experience from the perspective of you being able to do your job and for the guests being able to see what you are doing. I always set up so that I am facing the most guests and the main part of the room. The entertainment of watching you paint is the *live* part of this whole formula, so don't underestimate what you need to do to get situated for putting on the best show possible.

Once I arrive in the room where I'll be painting, I try to flag down one of my main venue contacts to make sure I set up in the right spot. It's terrible to unload all of your gear and set up only to find out you are supposed to be on the other side of the room (or that you're in the wrong room entirely). When I'm not able to confirm my location with the venue contact immediately on arrival, I strategically unpack and set my gear up for the least amount of hassle if I have to move.

Ideally you will have received photos of your location, the room, and/or a floor plan from your host prior to the event, so that you know where to go even if you can't find the banquet boss. If not, you'll want to stake out the room for the perfect spot. I've had times where I located a better view than what was originally anticipated and the floor plan could accommodate the change.

What do you need for the perfect spot? Stages and other elevated areas are the best of both worlds: you have a great view of all the action, and the guests have a clear view of the entertainment. However, stages are not as common in venues as you may think, and if there is musical entertainment, they are usually placed on the stage first.

Balconies are not ideal unless they are in a high-traffic area. While you have a gorgeous view of the room, nobody will be able to see what you are doing unless they happen to wander past you.

Think about the best unobstructed view you can get of the main scene that you need to paint.

It's also important to make sure you know where the DJ or band will be. I've set up only to have a late-arriving DJ place a stack of speakers in front of my designated spot.

Of course you likely can't set up front and center unless the hosts tell you to do so. And practical annoyances will also dictate your location. If you are outside, coverage from rain and sun is the most important consideration. While it may be absolutely beautiful to be placed at the foot of the aisle at a ceremony painting, if there are any clouds in the sky, that won't be your best option unless it's covered. Or, if you are a ginger like me, you may toast in the sun while you paint. If you are painting outside, you also need to consider the ground beneath you. If you are painting outside and the ground is uneven, you will need an easel with legs that can adjust in height.

The other most common consideration in technical placement is lighting. Are you going to be painting in the dark at all? If so, you'll need access to an electrical outlet to plug in your lights. Because of this, a spot that might have been ideal, like at the foot of the dance floor, may become a liability—you don't want to risk someone tripping on a long extension cord that you ran across the room and didn't secure properly. Better yet, consider getting battery-powered lights or a battery pack that you can plug into.

Finally, you may not want to be somewhere in the middle of traffic, because guests are often inebriated at events and you risk someone bumping into your easel or damaging the canvas.

Gear and Your Setup

Your gear is another key factor in setting up. In no specific order, here is a list of the materials and items you will need to perform a live painting.

Remember to adjust this list for your own medium's needs (for example, and artist using oil paint will need some different accessories than a watercolor artist).

- Easel
- Paint
- Brushes
- Receptacle for water or other liquids (varnish, mineral spirits, etc.)
- Palette
- Palette knives
- Rags or paper towels
- Canvas
- A plastic drop cloth
- A canvas drop cloth
- A place to lay out your paints (whether that's a table or by your feet)
- A suitcase to transport gear
- Signage
- Lighting
- Extension cord
- Camera tripods
- Business cards
- Stanchions
- A stool (if you sit while you paint)
- Water pitcher
- A sketch pad
- Receptacle for dirty liquid (depending on the requirements of your venue for disposal)

Now that you know what stuff you will need to have and exactly where you will be working, consider how you are actually going to set it up.

The amount of space you need to set up is going to vary widely based on your needs. I've seen some artists advertise that they only need a three-by-four-foot space. I've expanded my required space over the years to ten by ten feet, largely because of the COVID-19 pandemic. Whatever space you think you need, make sure it is included in your contract. I have had venues claim they have nowhere to put me, or venues that have tried to squeeze me into micro-sized spaces. If it's in your contract and your host fails to supply you with the space you need to do your job, you are covered if you can't proceed and they are at fault.

Once you've navigated the chaos of unloading, ensure that your spot meets all of your needs:

- You can see the space you are going to paint.
- You are covered from the elements.
- You have electricity access if needed.

Now what do you do first?

Unless you are painting outside, you'll need to first protect the immediate area where you will be painting. Put down your drop cloths. They aren't always pretty, but if aesthetics is a concern, purchase a new one for each event. Even if you are outside, don't assume the hosts don't want you to cover the area. Some people don't want to see paint on their patio or perfectly manicured lawn after the event.

I always use a plastic drop cloth underneath a thick canvas one; that way, even if I spill a whole mug of paint water, the surface beneath will be protected. The other reason drop cloths are handy are because they stake a claim, so to speak, to the area where you need to work. Some guests are aware enough to dodge your canvas for fear of getting paint on their fancy shoes.

The next thing you'll want to position is your easel. You'll want to consider what kind of a view you can give guests. I know it can be challenging, especially to a new Live Painter, to paint with your back to the scene. If that's the case, at least try to angle yourself so that people can see when they walk by. You never want to have your back fully to a wall.

Sometimes, if my setup allows, I'll start by facing the scene and just before the event starts I'll flip so that the "audience" is behind me and can watch as I paint.

I'm often asked what kind of easel to get, but the answer depends on the medium and size you work in. If your paintings are smaller, a good-quality plein air easel is a great investment. They are portable and have adjustable legs to accommodate uneven ground outside. They are also aesthetically pleasing—clients love them because they seem to embody the stereotypical "European fine artist" profile they tend to think of when they think of a painter, and they usually blend nicely into a formal setting because of their design's clean lines.

However, if you are painting on a larger canvas, steadiness will be the most important factor in terms of what easel to use. Unfortunately, larger-scale easels don't usually come with adjustable legs, so they can be problematic in outdoor setting, and they are not as adaptable as tripod easels. They also generally don't travel as well (the fact that they don't break down for travel is part of what makes them more reliable). Whenever I use my large-scale easel (a Mabef tilting lyre easel), we have to put the back seats down in my Subaru. I did take care to purchase a smaller large-scale easel, because they are heavy and you don't want to drag something heavier around than what it needs to be.

If you live or work in an urban location or are traveling to do destination events, you are probably going to need a smaller, portable easel. Regardless, I personally never use those cheap black metal easels. They fall apart and are only suitable for displaying lightweight work.

Okay. Your drop cloth is down and your easel is set up. Go ahead and put your canvas safely on the easel. Everything else in your setup revolves around what *you* need at hand when you paint. I used to not use a table—I liked adding the movement and drama of dropping paint tubes at my feet while I worked a wild brush. However, after doing 74,560 squats in the span of a few hours, I learned that using a table for my supplies is much easier on me the day after. I'm a messy painter, and so my messy table doesn't always present ideally, but it's the sacrifice I make to be able to walk in the morning.

On my table are my palette, brushes, paints, and water receptacle. A clip-on light is attached to the top of my easel, plugged into a power strip, which is usually plugged in to a thirty-foot extension cord (extra-long just in case). My phone charger is also plugged in to the power strip. An attachable tripod twists and bends around my easel and is one of the places I put my phone for reference photos while I paint. I can also set up my phone on the tripod to record video for a different point of view to add to a vlog or social media later. I keep my rags on the bottom rung of my easel in easy reach, and some business cards tucked into the easel's brush lip and on the table.

I often have a second camera tripod set up for a wider angle, which is where I catch most of the footage of my painting process for videos. Then, I put out my signs and my stanchions. I used to not use stanchions, as I liked being able to keep an open, friendly space where onlookers could get close to the painting. The COVID-19 pandemic unfortunately changed this for me, and stanchions became a way to protect myself and social distance while still being in a crowded room. The good news is that there are also fewer incidents of handsy dudes getting too friendly while I paint.

Keep your signage simple. I use the same social media handle on all platforms, and it's a way to remember and spell, so when people ask about me I point to any of the @thelivepainter signs and they usually follow me on the spot. It's the best way to naturally grow an online audience that will feel passionate about supporting you. Everyone likes to be able to say "Hey, I know that person!" when they see a video.

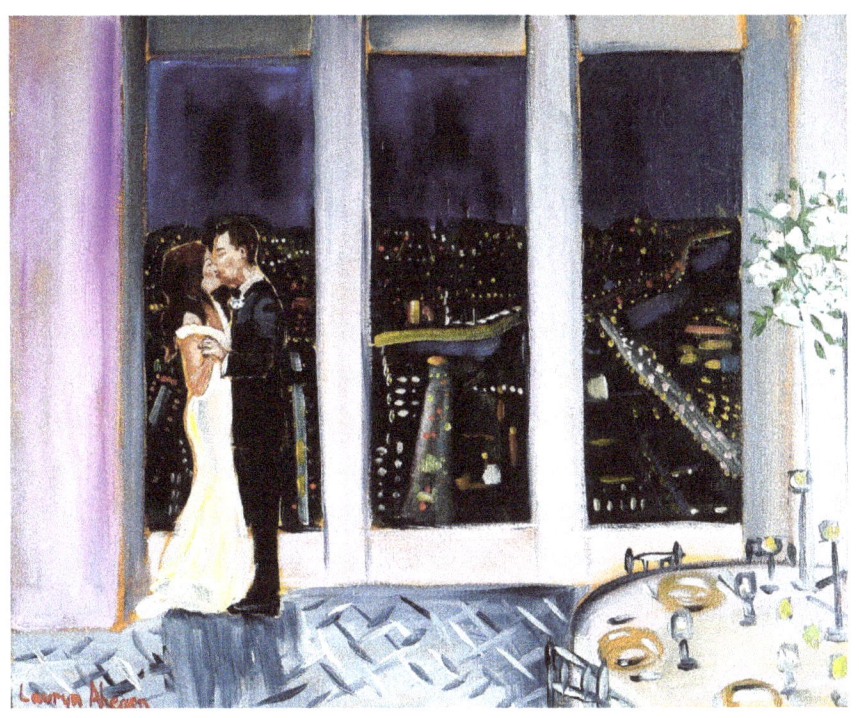

9

PLAN, THEN PAINT

You've arrived at your event. You've navigated the parking, unloading, and setting up, and everything is ready to go. All of your technical needs are met, and you have a view of the room that is clear and will be the foundation of the painting composition. What's next?

It depends on your medium and how fast you paint. You need to have an idea of how long it takes you to complete a painting to determine how early you should arrive at the venue and what you should paint prior to the start of the event, if anything.

It takes me four to seven hours to paint a live event. The larger the canvas is, of course, the longer it takes to complete. While I do not consider myself a "speed painter," I am usually able to finish the painting of the event before the end of the event. This is partially due to strategizing when to begin the painting.

Considering that the average wedding reception lasts four to five hours, I am usually able to complete the bulk of the painting during the actual time of the performance. However, I prefer to finish painting a little on the early side so that guests have time to *ooh* and *ahh* at the painting before the event is over, and also so the painting has a little time to dry before it needs to be transported. Considering all these factors, I usually begin painting about one hour prior to the event. You don't want to start so early that the guests miss too much of the performance—remember, half of the reason you are painting at an event is so the guests can witness you paint live.

I know that the idea of learning how to paint something from a written book may sound difficult, which is why I am giving you a theory perspective. In this chapter I discuss the formula for painting live, but I am unable to visually show you. That's why I offer streaming sessions at the Live Painter Academy. My sessions offer the opportunity to demonstrate in greater depth the techniques I talk about, and if you are local you can even get to observe me at a live event, and then have me at your side during *your* gig. It's like having the ultimate private art tutor. It's a worthy business investment, because doing just one event as a Live Painter can generate a payout of several thousand dollars. You can go to my website, TheLivePainter.com or LivePainterAcademy.com to learn more.

As you gain experience, you will learn how to tell when you are "on schedule" and when you are behind in your painting process. I know that by the time the guests start to arrive, I should at least be making progress on the background. If it's a smaller painting, I only have to finish the ground color before the guests enter. If I know painting the guests is going to be more involved—for example, the wedding couple has a very large wedding party and they want everyone to be included—I try to make sure I'm wrapping up the background by the time the guests walk in. How early you start and what you complete prior to guests entering really depends on you, and the only way to figure out what it is you need is practice. This is why you will practice painting at home many times before you paint a live event.

Composition and Ground Color

Before you lay a brush to your canvas, you need to figure out two basic things: the basic composition and your ground color.

When considering composition, you have to look at both what is before your eyes now and what may be in front of you later. The room composition will usually not change during the event (though the coloring might—more on that momentarily). However, when starting your painting, you will not know what the room looks like when the guests arrive. Because of this, you need to use a little bit of psychic ability to start your painting. If you know that your guests will be sitting at tables in the images, you need to keep in mind the space where the guests will be physically located if you are painting tables before the guests are present. You may not want to spend a lot of time on the details of a particular table, for example, if once the guests arrive you won't be able to see what is on the table anyway. I can't tell you how many times I labored over the tiny details of a table setting only to paint over it with imagery of a guest sitting with their back to me.

You also need to decide fairly early on where you will place the guests of honor. In a live painting, these folks are usually your client or the family of the client, depending on who hired you. They are the bride and groom, the couple celebrating their fiftieth anniversary, the bar or bat mitzvah, the quinceañera queen, or the mother, father, and baby. In the case of a first dance live wedding painting, there is some flexibility in where you will paint the couple on your canvas. While some artists prefer a dead center composition, with the couple in the front and the rest of the guests around them in a sort of semicircle, if I am painting a live event, I find that painting the guests of honor off to one side or the other of the painting creates a more engaging composition, as long as I am able to balance it.

I like to put the wedding cake or a glimpse of floral arrangements on the opposite side of the painting, which creates variety in the foreground and background and strengthens the composition overall, while also capturing special details the wedding couple will appreciate having in their paintings. Now the wedding cake or glimpse of florals from the top of a table may not really be in the bottom right corner of your view, but that's the magic of live painting. Unlike event photographers, we have the power to pick and choose.

To help you solidify your composition before you begin painting, I strongly recommend drawing a quick sketch on a paper pad for how you will set up the painting. This is not something that you should spend more than five minutes on. Some artists will sketch out the composition on their canvas in addition to or instead of drawing on a pad of paper. They might use pencil, charcoal, or a neutral painting color on top of the ground wash.

Even if your painting style is abstract, an understanding of perspective is paramount for a live event painter. If you aren't strong with perspective, or it's been a while, there are many resources online that can teach you how to approach it.

You need to determine your vanishing points and horizon for the composition, and if you are painting inside of a room, getting the lines of the ceiling, walls, and any architectural details close to life is important for laying a strong foundation in your composition. I have used both painter's tape and rulers to lay out my most important corners, long lines, and horizons when I paint because I find crisper edges help rein-force proper perspective, even if your brush strokes are loose.

If you've taken any formal drawing or painting courses, then you've probably used some sort of grid approach or viewfinder in the past to layout a composition for a work of art. If I'm having difficulty capturing the right angles of a room, I use a simple cheat: I shoot a photo of the room with my camera that shows the composition I want. Having a two-dimensional reference as I lay out the perspective helps me envision a solid structure for the layout of the room on the canvas. You can also use traditional viewfinders or an artist's drawing scope if you need a little extra help. The guests won't consider using tools for good angles "cheating."

Painting a scene that takes place outside is sometimes easier than painting an interior because there are fewer lines and angles that must be precise for an accurate rendering of the scene—unless you are painting a nearby structure like a manor home or a barn. You do have to prop-erly convey distance in a composition like this. For example, if you are painting an outdoor wedding ceremony, it's important that the wedding couple in the distance is the right size compared to the sizes of the guests looking on, from both near and far points of the view in the painting.

Coloring

Your composition is not the only thing that should be planned ahead. You also need to consider the painting's coloring before you begin. The two most important factors in this decision includes lighting and what your client wants.

Start with what your client wants. Weddings often have a color theme chosen by the bride. It's pretty well known that most brides coordinate the colors of the flowers and the dresses, and sometimes other decorations, special accents, and even the cake. Ask your clients before the event if there are any color themes that should be represented strongly. Likely for a wedding, the client will think of this event color palette they've chosen. But for you, the colors of the event have depth far beyond coordinating flowers and dresses. You need to choose the tone of the entire scene. The best way to find out what tone your client wants is to ask them beforehand to use words that describe their ideal finished painting. If they tell me they want a "light romantic" look versus a "bright, fun representation" my color palette is going to be completely different.

Fine artists often don't like to think of themselves as being used to match the couch to the pillow in the room the painting will hang, but this is also a practical consideration for giving your client a product they love. Sometimes they don't know where the finished painting will hang, and that's okay. If they do know, ask them about any colors they might like to see in the painting that could help with their interior design later. I admit I do not ask all of my clients this question. If I get the sense that it could open a Pandora's box of demands, I skip it. However if I sense the client will be reasonable and work with me, I try.

For outdoor events, or events inside venues with a lot of windows or natural lighting, you must consider if the event will be changing from day to night while you paint. This small detail will completely change your approach to foundational coloring on the canvas. For example, I once painted in a venue where the center of the ballroom had a large window that covered the entire back wall of the composition, with a view of a barn and the ocean. When I began painting, it was just before sunset, but I would be painting most of the event in the night. I needed to quickly decide if I should be painting with daylight from the window, or if I should be painting as if the sun had set. This is something you can discuss with your clients beforehand also—for example, a wedding may only have the colors of a sunset for ten minutes, but that may be what the client wants you to capture for the entire paining. If your client has no preferences, then you need to decide spontaneously at the event which way you will go. You need to essentially predict light, shadows, and the changing colors affected by them.

Another important factor to consider when choosing your ground colors is whether an inside venue will have any up-lighting or light shows. Up-lighting is when a venue has lights reflecting up onto the walls, and they can be done in different colors. I find that for most of my indoor venues, the yellow chandelier lighting and overhead lights are turned up high while the vendors set up. However, the lights are eventually dimmed, and up-lighting could change an entire room from a general yellow light to a fluorescent blue, magenta, pink, or any other color. Your best way to work with up-lighting is to discuss it with the venue coordinator or party planner ahead of time. If you are unable to confirm with them, I will often ask the DJ if there is any up-lighting or show, because the DJs are often contributing some sort of colored lighting to the party, and they may already know about the lighting or be able to tell you about the special effects that they plan to use. You can also check in with photographers and videographers—they usually are familiar with the lighting situation because this affects their work product as much as it affects yours.

Once you know what the lighting is when you start and will be later, you can choose a ground color for your painting. Sometimes, the ground color I use is not actually part of the lighting of the room at all but is based on a preference made by the client. I once painted an indoor wedding ceremony where my bride told me she wanted the painting to have a lot of green in it, as this would match her living room. The room itself was not green at all in terms of decor or lighting. I used a green ground color, which let me give an overall undertone of green in the painting, and I was able to give her the look she wanted while also remaining true to the event and providing a beautiful finished product.

It's important to think about whether you want a warm or cool painting for the end result when you pick the ground color. Because so many indoor nighttime venues have an orange glow to their lighting, I find myself using Indian yellow or Naples yellow as common grounds in more neutral settings, especially if there is a lot of wood in the room. As I layer my paint, having that warm ground color helps the overall product to glow, and it also helps me capture the brightness of light fixtures and reflective surfaces later on.

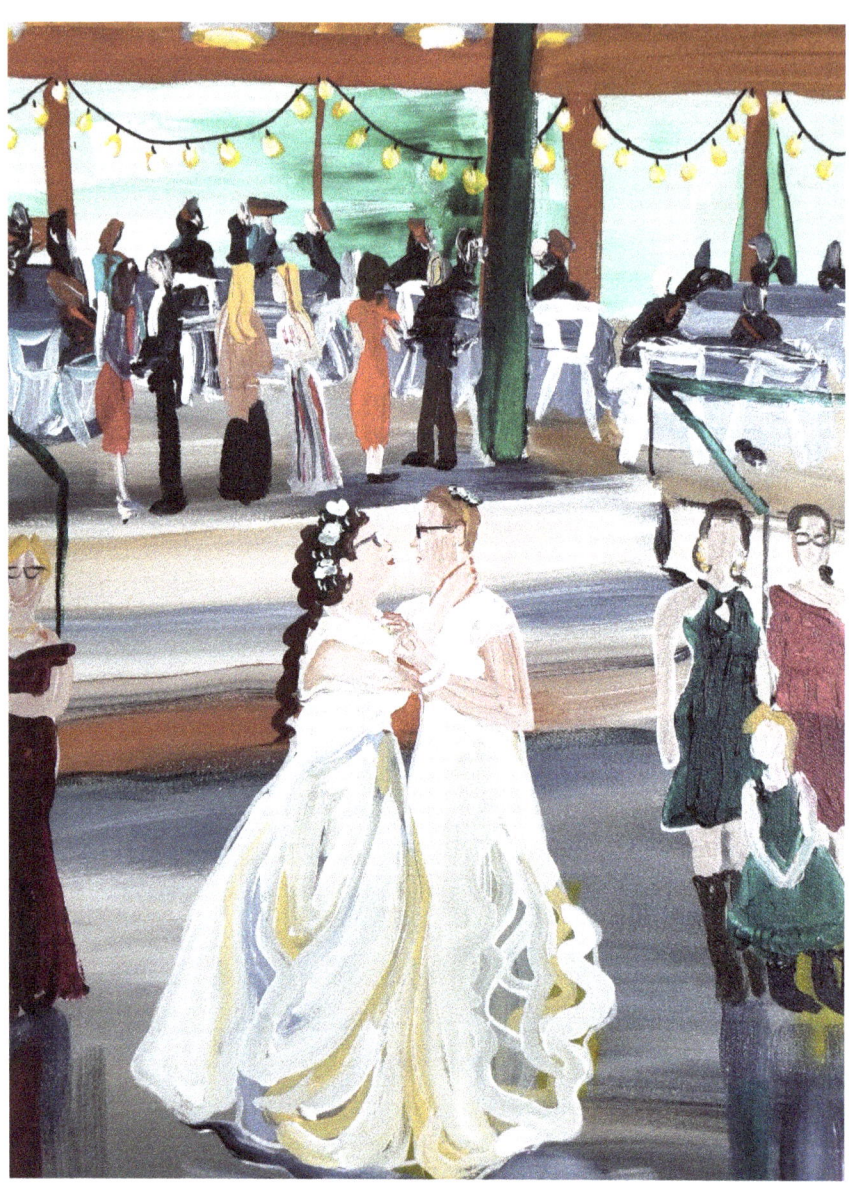

10

FINALLY PAINTING

Once I lay out my basic composition and ground color, I'm ready to start to work the painting. This part of my process is difficult to explain in writing, but if you join me for sessions online or in person you will be able to see step-by-step demonstrations of each part of my process for different common compositions and event scenarios.

My first task is painting the background. As I said before, I try to be either partially or fully finishing up the background by the time the guests begin to arrive. Which end of the spectrum of completion I need to be up to really depends on how much time I need for a painting. Generally speaking, though, the more of the process the guests are able to see as you paint, the more exciting the performance is for them, because they can see the full beginning-to-end experience of you working your magic.

Taking Reference Photos

The most common composition for wedding couples is the first dance. Usually, when the reception starts, the MC or DJ will introduce the bridal party. If your wedding couple requested that certain people's likeness be included in the finished product, this is your chance to learn who is who and to take reference photos as they enter and then again as they line up around the dance floor for the first dance. These photos will be lifesavers for you later when you need to paint your guests in.

Once the wedding couple is introduced, take as many photos as possible of them during the dance (assuming that is the moment you are painting). Afterward, you will be choosing one of these photos to use as your main reference for painting your guest(s) of honor. Even if the main moment of a wedding painting is not the first dance, you will likely want to take pictures because you can use their positioning in other compositions if needed. For example, they can be holding each other the way they danced when it's time to cut the cake in your painting.

When I first started live event painting, I was afraid guests would consider it "cheating" if they caught me looking at reference photos on my phone while I paint. I've since learned that most do not notice or care. They are too busy looking at your work and enjoying the party to look around at what tools you are using. I do take care to not to make the device I'm using for my reference photos too obvious. Some artists use tablets on special tripods so that they have a large screen to reference as they paint, but I prefer to use my own phone as the smaller screen is more discreet. Ultimately, though, you have nothing to hide, because photographing moments you need is not cheating. Live events have important but fleeting moments that need to be captured, and unless you have an incredible photographic memory, you will need something to look at to provide the clients with the finished product they asked for.

If you are an artist who finishes the work once you are in the studio, reference photos are not optional. You will need them later to be able to finish your work. Also, even if you plan to finish the painting on site, in the event that you are unexpectedly unable to finish for any reason, you have the photos as a backup.

It is extremely important to be aware of your surroundings while taking reference photos, especially at weddings for first dances. You need to be able to take clear, unobstructed photos of the first dance, so don't be shy about getting to the front of the crowd. However, you want to take care that you are not blocking the wedding photographer or videographer, and you also want to make sure you are not in their shots. The wedding couple will not want a photo of their first dance with you standing out holding your camera up in the background. To avoid this faux pas, I usually try to stay behind the photographers and slightly to their side, so that I can see and take clear photos but that I am also not in their way or in the professional shots.

Guests who have not yet seen you by your easel may give you odd looks when you move to the front to take photos. They may think you are a friend or relative behaving self-importantly. I do need to do my job, but I try to also be aware of where guests are standing, especially family members. I try not to block their view, and when I take photos close to the dance floor I often go down on one knee just as the professional photographers do, so that anyone behind me can see over me.

Finding Your Rhythm

Once you have these all-important photos of the bridal party's entrance and first dance, you can go back to the easel and get to work again. This is the moment where I usually feel like I'm ready to fully get into a rhythm when I proceed.

Now that guests are present, you will be able to further solidify your composition. For first dance imagery, I ask wedding couples if they want the first dance painted exactly as it occurred, just as a single photo may represent who was standing where, or if they would like me to create a more spontaneous composition that includes wedding highlights. I am happy to say most couples trust me enough to leave it up to me, and painting a highlight and first dance combo is my favorite painting to do because it gives me the freedom and flexibility I need to make the best possible final product.

When you are finished painting the background, it will be time to paint the guests. You must know if you are painting a crowd on a dance floor, a crowd sitting at tables, or a combination of the two. I try to work from background to foreground, regardless of the layout I am going with.

The only time I break this self-imposed ruled is when I am painting the guests of honor. In my example of painting a first dance, this means you need to decide early on where the wedding couple will be having their first dance on the canvas. I will usually paint some first layers for the guests evenly on the painting, and then before adding details to the guests, I change my focus to painting the wedding couple and guests of honor. Because they are almost always in the foreground, this can make it a little tricky later when I fill in the guests around them. But I start with the wedding couple because (a) this is the most important part of the painting for the clients who are paying you, (b) they will require the most detail and attention since you need them to be perfect, and for me that means adding layers as they dry over time, and (c) if you do not finish the painting during the event, the clients and guests will be happy to see at least a close-to-finished rendering of the most important people.

Painting the Guests of Honor

I take my time painting the guests of honor, and while I try to concentrate on their detail before I spend too much time on other aspects of the painting, you learn as a professional artist that the best paintings are worked evenly all over. And so I tend to bounce around from spending time on painting a strong start of the wedding couple, and then filling them in with more detail as I begin to add detail to the rest of the painting.

Painting Guests in the Background

Painting guests in the background is the freest part of the painting process with my particular approach and style. Because my live works are in an abstract impressionist style, the guests in the background of the painting are usually made up of layers of basic shapes and color, giving the cumulative illusion of a crowd in motion once the painting is complete. The guests the clients want to include in the work but who are not the main focus of the painting are often painted later in my process. This is because they need to be painted closer to the foreground over my more generic abstract crowd. These guests are what give your "crowd" specificity and form. While these guests will not have the level of minute detail I include for the wedding couple, I make sure they are recognizable and distinct from the rest of the crowd. Coloring of skin, hair, and clothing is the most important aspect of creating their presence in the work, and their placement in the work is the next most important thing. You want to make sure, for example, that the parents of the bride and groom are standing together, with the couples appropriately placed. You don't want to paint the bride's mother with the groom's father accidentally, and divorced parents may be unhappy with being painted next to each other.

On Your Way

At this point, your painting should be well on its way. If it's not close to being finished, then at least the final product should be able to be imagined by the average non-artist based on the progress you've made so far. Once you have the most crucial elements of the room, the guests in the background, the wedding couple or guests of honor in the foreground, and the important guests recognizably painted and appropriately located in the composition, the remainder of your time will be spent heightening the detail of what is already painted, and adding standout details to the work.

Standout details refers to two things. The first is making your more generic guests more recognizable. This is one of my favorite parts of a live event painting, because the pressure is off and most of the important aspects of the painting are finished, so now I can pick out guests from the crowd and paint their likeness into the work. I tend to home in on guests who are wearing colors or patterns that make them distinct, because representing them in the painting helps reinforce the spontaneity of the work. It's also the best way to get guests involved in the art. They will be delighted to pick themselves out of the crowd in your painting because they see their blue dress with white flowers and blond up-do, or they see their brightly colored tie with their familiar posture. It's always a little harder to make men stand out, but putting them next to their brightly dressed partner helps. Other times, you will find someone who stands out because they are particularly tall or wearing distinctive suspenders or the like. If you have enough time before the end of the event, you can add as many specific guests as you want to the composition. The more you are able to include, the more your finished product will show the unique presentation of the event you are painting.

And there is even more to this standout portion of your painting: As with any good painting, there is always more detail, more layers, or more color to add. It is rare that you will have the opportunity to overwork your live painting during an event, so do not worry about this happening. If you have time, use that time wisely to add as many layers and colors and small details as you can to fully customize the painting and make it a strong finished work. When I am discussing an upcoming event with couples, I note that there is always something more for me to add to the painting. You will not need to look hard to find what else to add once you get the bulk of your painting down on canvas.

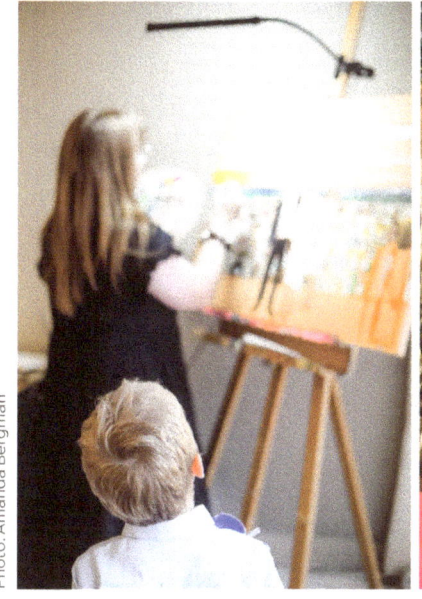
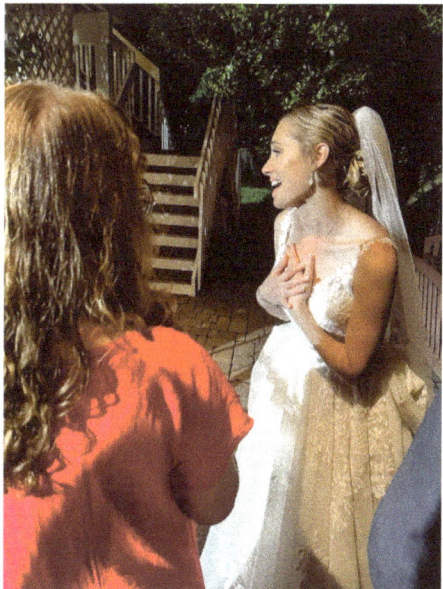

11

INTERACTING WITH GUESTS

The painting you were hired to create is the main focus of your mission for any live event painting. But don't forget that the performance is also a big part of your job as a live event painter. Even if you've chosen to brand your performance as a moody and aloof artist deeply involved in the painting process, you must be able to acknowledge guests who approach you and answer their questions while you work.

Guests at the Easel

When guests approach your easel, some will be interested in talking to you, while others will be content to watch and or comment on the performance to their friends. You will find over time that guests ask the same types of questions at every event, and even if you are shy you will be able to pull up your practiced answer without losing focus.

The most common questions I am asked by onlookers include:

"When did you start the painting?"

"Will you finish it tonight?"

"How long have you been doing this for?"

"What are you painting?"

"Am I going to be in the picture?"

Guests also will ask various other questions about your background and experience as an artist. They're not asking these questions to be nosy. They most likely have never seen a live event painter before and will be fascinated by everything about you and your presence at the event.

You may have some difficulty discussing the performance with guests because you are pressed for time. Consider the moments you take to speak with guests as part of the time it takes you to complete a painting and factor that into your arrival and start time. This way you won't feel pressure to brush off interested guests because you are in a rush to get your paint on the canvas.

Make sure to make eye contact as much as possible with guests who come to speak with you. Remember that every guest you meet is a potential client or referral. It will be a long time before people forget seeing your performance, if they ever forget, and any time someone they know is getting married they will be guaranteed to mention the Live Painter they saw at so-and-so's wedding, and how amazing it was. You want to be open and friendly. You'll find that guests tend to make the same jokes over time just as they'll ask similar questions—often the joke will be about making them more attractive in the painting than they are in real life. Find a charming way to respond to these jokes that does not insult guests. For example, when someone asks laughingly, "Can you paint me thinner?" I give them a big smile and say, "The magic of live event painting is that you can paint anything you want!" Other jokes I often get are "Hey, which one is me?" and "Do I have to stay still all night?" Try not to roll your eyes at these, even if you've heard the joke a million times. How you mingle with guests is part of your brand, and you want to respond to the more predictable banter with an on-point one-liner response that only makes the audience adore you more.

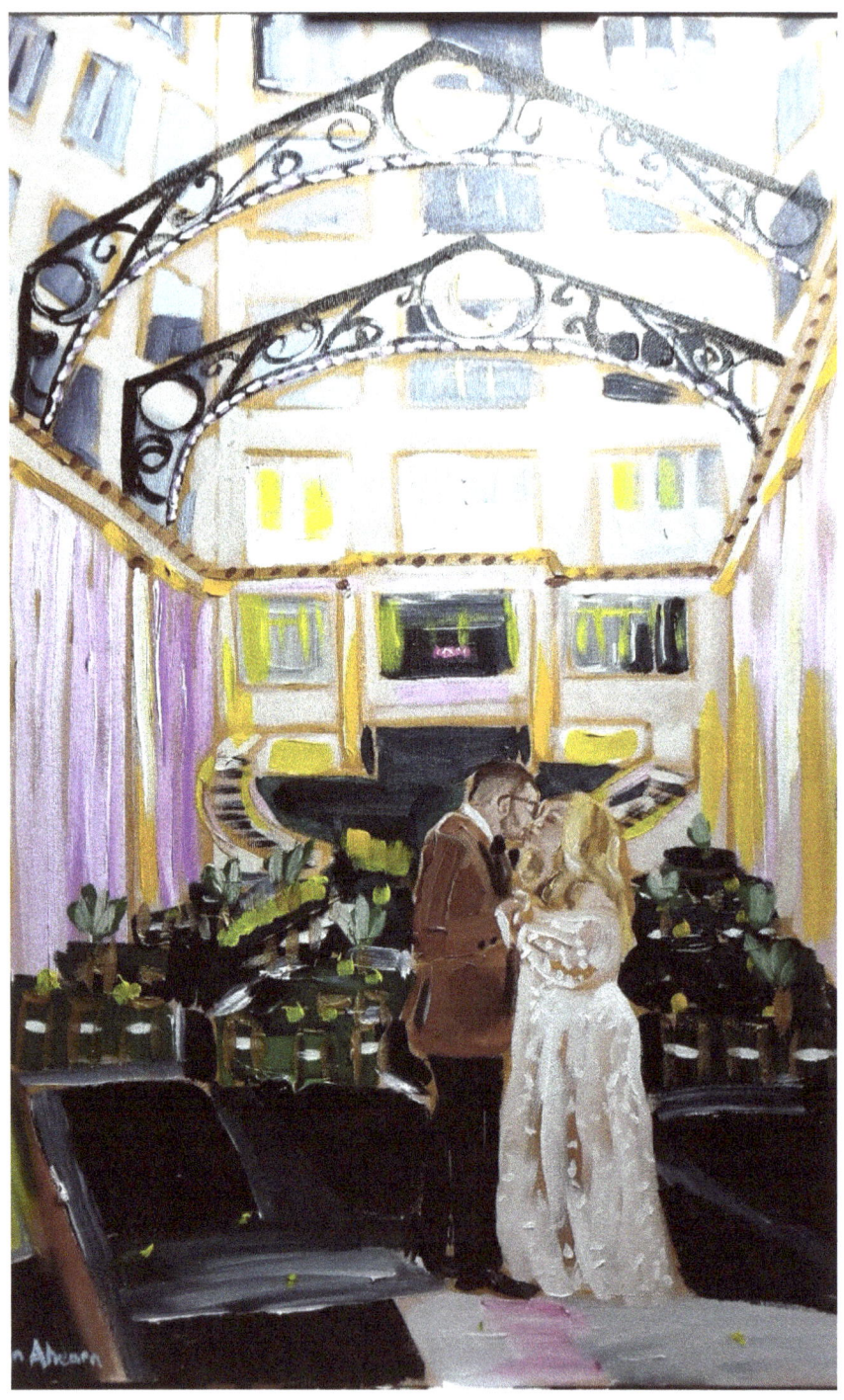

12

TAKING BREAKS DURING THE EVENT

While performing is part of your job as a live event painter, you should not be expected to paint nonstop during the event. I make sure when I book an event that my client understands that they may not see me at the easel every time they look at it. Not only do we as human beings with physical needs need to step away for the bathroom or food, but there are functional aspects in the painting process of stepping away from the easel. Sometimes we need to wash brushes, sometimes a layer of paint needs to dry a little, and sometimes our eyes need a break so we can see more clearly when we work and spot problem areas on the canvas. I include this information in my contracts but inform the client that I will be at my easel performing as much as I can. Usually the guests of honor are so busy that they are not keeping track of your coming and going anyway.

Eating and Drinking

If an event is four or more hours and food is being served, I always make sure the client intends to feed me as well. It's standard in the event industry for vendors to be fed, but not everyone knows this, and they may need the reminder to include you (and your artist assistant, if you have one) in their vendor head count to the venue. When setting up before the event, try to find out from the venue host or waitstaff how to know when the vendor meals are ready and where they will be located. Too many times the live event painter is forgotten at their easel and doesn't find out their meal has been served until it's gone cold—and that's if anything is left.

A common debate among event vendors is whether it's appropriate to drink at a wedding or not, especially in an open-bar scenario. Most vendors will tell you that they do not drink at work. Live event painters can be an odd sort of exception, though. First, part of the artist's stereotypical image is holding a glass of wine while they work. Live painters are also vendors that fall into a sort of pseudo guest role. Think of the role of the governess in the nineteenth century—they were not considered servants, but they were not part of the family either. Live painters are an odd sort of parallel to this type of position in the event. Some painters say that they read the crowd to decide if they may have a drink or not. I am more comfortable having an alcoholic drink with my dinner than at my easel. If you do have a drink at your easel, be careful where you keep your drink and your paint water so you don't mix them up!

If you do choose to drink at an event, remember to be professional. It is *never* appropriate to be drunk in a paid performance setting.

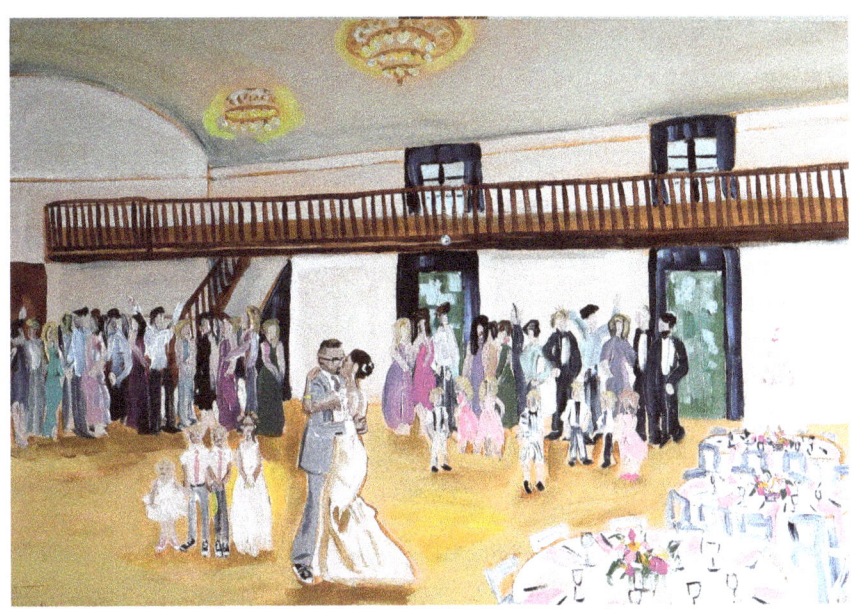

13

FINISHING
THE PAINTING

Not all artists finish paintings at events. Some paintings may not be finished due to technical reasons, like the paint needs to dry more before final touches can be applied. Some paintings may not be finished because it is simply not part of the artist's process to finish a painting at the event.

Even if you tend to finish your paintings before the event ends, make sure to have a contingency arrangement with your client, both verbally and in the contract. In the off chance that you are unable to finish, will you bring it to your studio to finish it for free? Is there an extra fee? What about getting the finished painting to the client? Will they pick it up, or will you deliver? Does it cost extra to deliver? How long will it be after the event before the client can expect the finished product? All of these considerations must be decided beforehand in writing.

When is the Painting Finished?

If you do plan to finish the painting at the event, when is the painting considered "finished"? Who decides that the painting is finished? Is it you or is it the client, or is it open to discussion? I also include this in my contract, which says that I decide if the painting is finished but that I will take the client's opinion into consideration. I could be a dictator and insist I'm done, but if a client is not happy, do I really want to leave them unhappy? But the boundary does need to be identified because some clients will never be satisfied—it's just who they are. You need to be protected with the right to say, "no more."

Once the painting is declared finished, make sure to identify in your contract that you are no longer responsible for the well-being of the painting. If you inform a couple that the painting is completed and they agree (getting at least their verbal confirmation is very important!), and then once you pack up and leave the venue damages it, you need to ensure you are not on the hook for making another painting for free or refunding their payment.

Some artists create a show out of declaring the painting finished. They do a special unveiling with the help of the DJ and a photo op with the happy couple, and some do a sort of "christening" by enjoying a Champagne toast in front of the painting. All of these are fun, and the images will be a great addition to your website and social media.

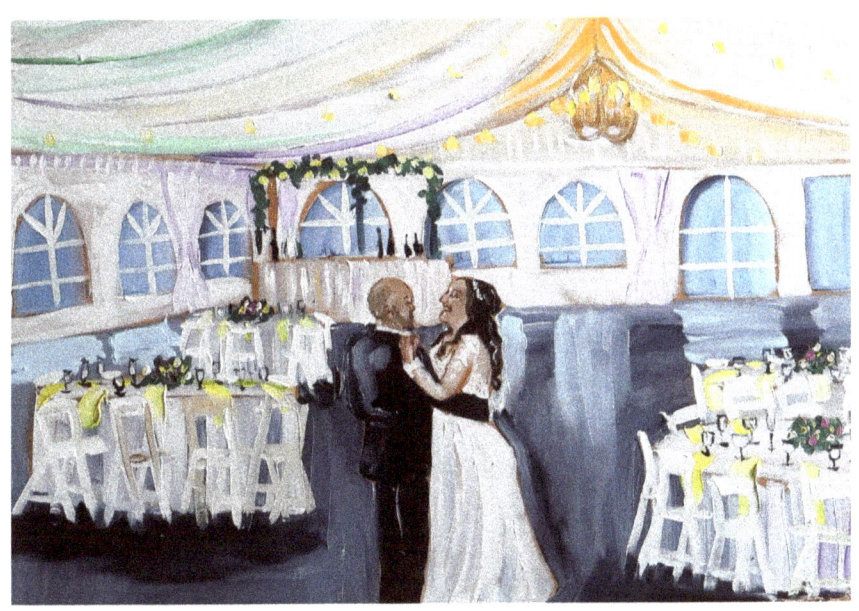

14

MAKING YOUR EXIT

The painting is finished—or the event is wrapping up and you are taking the canvas back to your studio. It's time to pack up and get out of there. You may or may not be doing this while the event is still going on or while guests are filing out themselves. Because of this I do my breakdown in the most aesthetically pleasing way possible. I pack up everything but the painting on the easel and any signs or business cards that direct people to my website or contact info. This way, guests can look at the finished product, take pictures, tag me on social media, and so on while I pack away the rest of my gear.

I wait as long as I possibly can to pack up the easel and the painting (and the light, if the room is dark). When it's time to finally make my exit, I break down the easel. If I'm leaving the painting at the venue for the clients, I include a cheap aluminum easel for show that I leave with the painting. If you aren't doing this, I recommend either putting it in a highly visible but safe place like on top of a table in the area you were painting in, or if there is no other choice you prop it against a wall somewhere where it will not drip on the venue's property. Sometimes I use the plastic drop cloth to protect the area. You may also be able to work with the venue coordinator if you found they were helpful.

Getting the Painting Home

If you are taking the painting with you and it is not fully dry, it goes without saying that you need to be very careful transporting it home. This aspect of your process may play into your decision of how large your painting offerings will be or what medium you decide to use. For me, if the painting is large, I lay my easel across my flipped-down backseat and trunk and affix the canvas onto the easel with nothing nearby that could roll or puncture it.

Cleaning Up

You must be absolutely meticulous about leaving your painting space exactly as you left it. This means cleaning up any garbage. You'll be happy at this point that you laid out a layer of plastic and canvas drop cloth if there were any spills or splashes during your painting. This makes cleanup very easy.

Be careful about where you dump your paint water. Some pigments are toxic, and the plastics in acrylics will clog drains and cause problems for water treatment plants. Additionally, some venues may have an environmental situation where the water can't be discarded on site. If this is the case you should bring a receptacle that you can use to transport the water back to your studio, such as a jar with a tight lid.

Getting Paid

Once everything is cleaned up, packed up, and spotless, and the painting is safely wherever it is supposed to be, it's time to leave—but not before you check in with your clients and get paid (if you did not retrieve the balance prior to the event). *Never leave an event without making sure you have the money that was due to you.* Some Live Painters follow the rule of not even starting the event until they have the money due to them. I personally found it challenging to collect my final payment at the end of weddings because the happy couple is usually having fun. It's difficult not to feel awkward when you interrupt their dancing with friends on the biggest day of their lives and ask for a check.

Because of all of this, I now require the final payment before the start of the event, if not before the date of the event.

Final To-Dos

Even if you've been paid, you don't want to leave the event without saying goodbye to your clients. Also make sure to check in with any venue hosts if you want to network with them. Give them your card and ask for theirs. Make sure they know that you can be their live painting preferred vendor if they are interested.

If the painting is coming home with you, you will need to coordinate delivery with your client. You may choose to offer free pickup and delivery with a fee, based on how far the client lives from you. Painters who do destination weddings will need to professionally ship the finished product to the client. Make sure to factor shipping costs into your fee if you are not including the option to add it as a separate fee in your contract, or you may find yourself losing a precious chunk of revenue. *Always* insure the work of art for its full value if you are shipping the canvas or hiring someone else to deliver it.

The Live Painter™

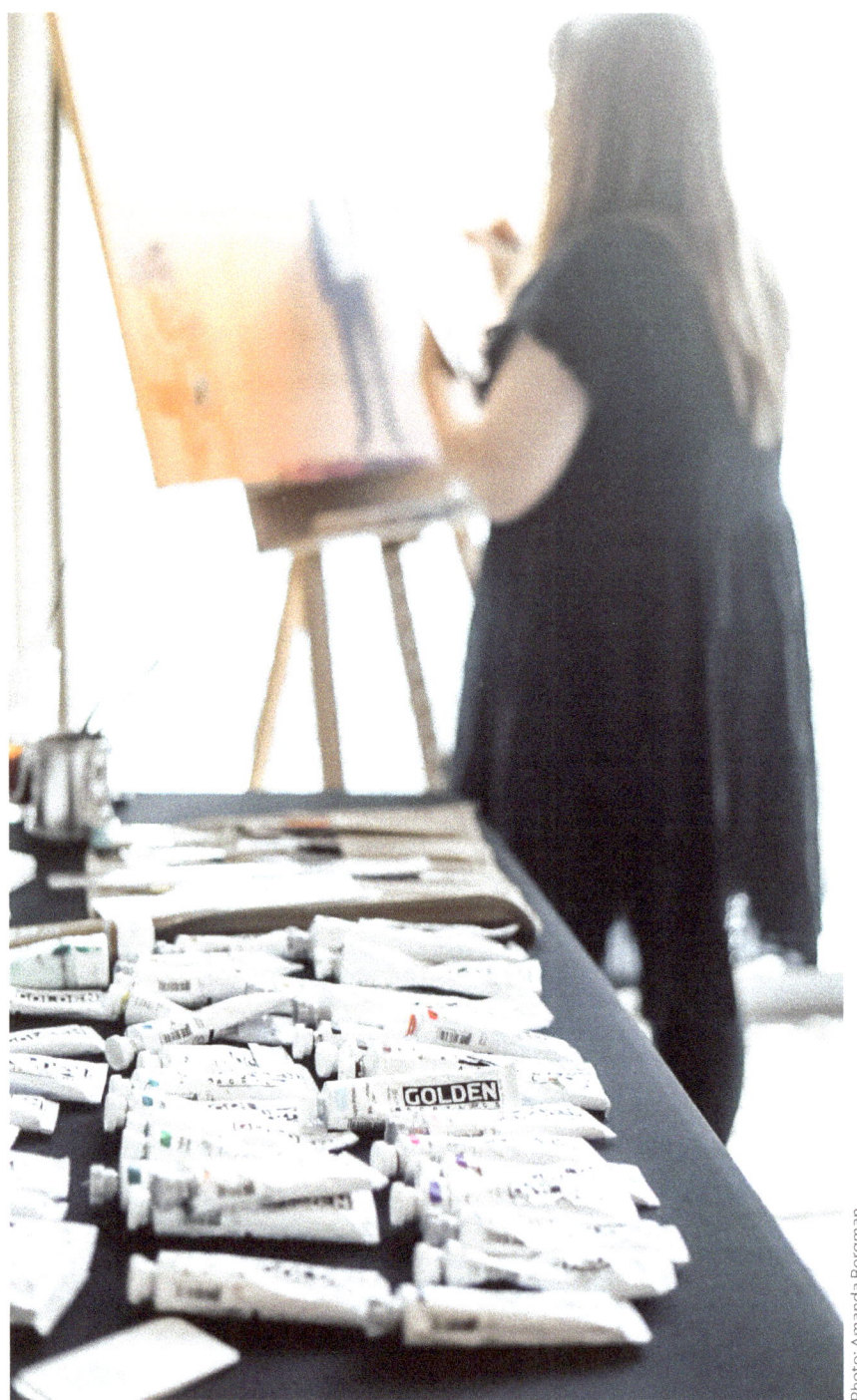

15

STAYING ORGANIZED

Staying organized can be a challenge for anyone, but artists in particular are known to struggle with the business end of art. That's one of the reasons I wrote this book—to help artists like you get it together so you can make money while gifting the world with your creations. Organizing the business end of your affairs includes budgeting, electronic filing on your cloud, supply inventory, invoicing, accounting, marketing, responding to inquiries, and more. It's important to develop a system that creates a logical workflow for you to follow from the first inquiry to following up after the event. To help you stay organized, here are two small checklists for before and after your events:

Before the Event

- Respond promptly to inquiries.
- Invoice and receive payments, including deposits.
- Create a spreadsheet or Word document that lists all your upcoming events and includes client names, contact info, the details of the event package they purchased from you, and any balance they may owe.

- Organize your pre-event inquiry forms so that you can easily locate them when it's time to hit the road.
- Make sure to retrieve the signed copy of the contract and then file your contract, both the signed and unsigned versions, so you can easily locate them.
- Make travel arrangements in advance—you don't want to scramble for a hotel because the only hotel within twenty miles of the venue is already booked up by party guests.

After the Event

- Follow up with your client about their satisfaction.
- Request a review if appropriate.
- Request any photos of the event that include you that they would be willing to share.
- Update your books to reflect payments you received from the event's completion.
- Update your website and social media accounts with photos and video from the event.

PART FOUR:

Onward and Upward

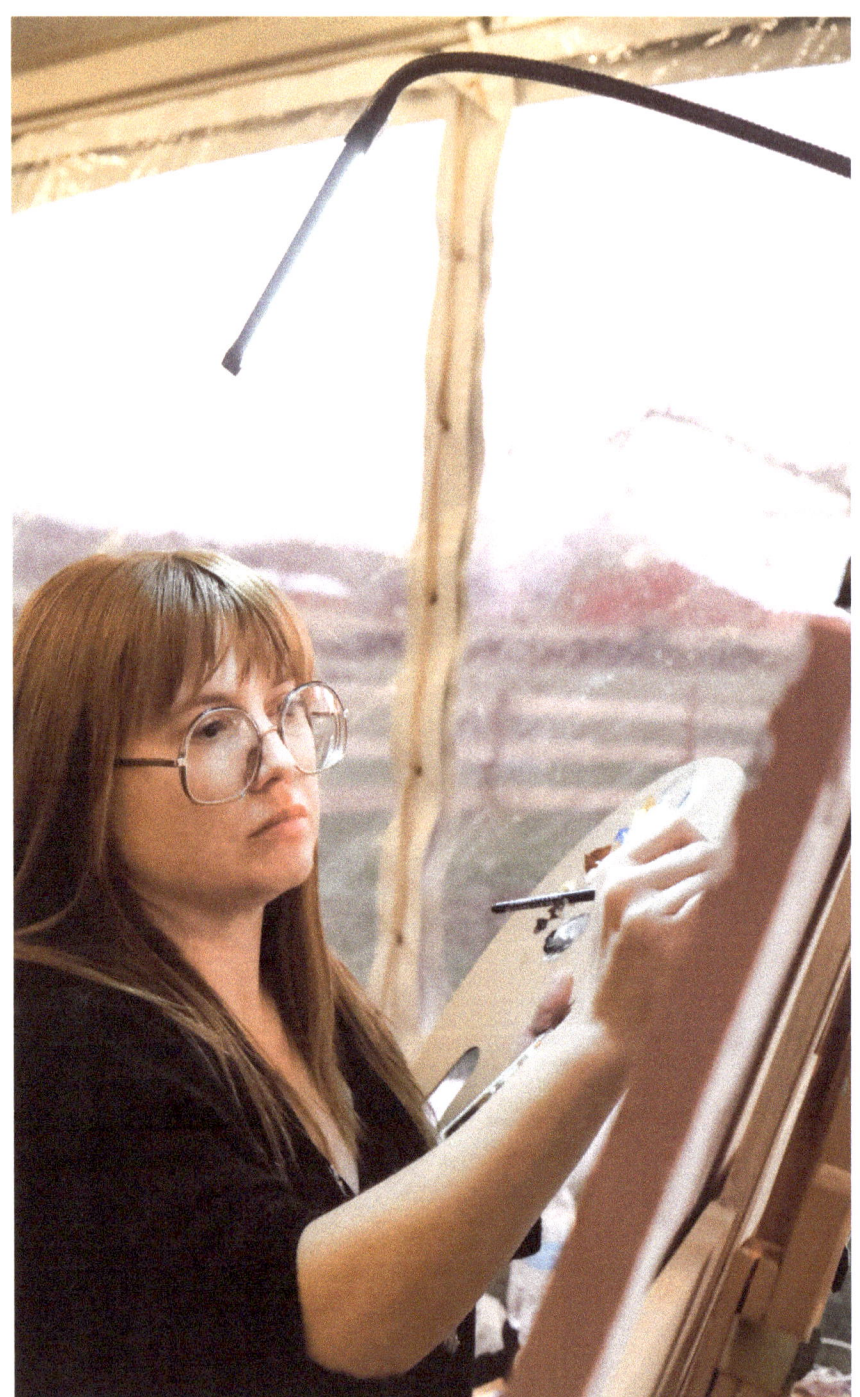

16

DEALING WITH COMMON CHALLENGES

Because live event painting is such a unique form of art and entertainment, it can be hard to find mentors to learn from. If you decide to work with me as your teacher and coach after reading this book, I will personally be able to guide you through issues when you encounter them at events. Otherwise you will unfortunately learn the hard lessons yourself and get guidance on dealing with them from this book.

Here are some trouble spots you may run into. Ideally, this information will help you navigate awkward situations in the future. Note that a number of these issues can be covered in your formal agreement with the client. I suggest you consult with a trusted attorney to draft an agreement that works best for you, or subscribe to an online legal service.

Honoring Your Style *and* What Your Clients Want

Sometimes, no matter how strong your brand is and how clear you are about what a client can expect, they may still be disappointed with the end result. The best way to avoid this rookie error is to ask your client plenty of questions about what they envision the finished work will look like. I have multiple questions in my booking intake form that screen for a client's preferences and expectations. (See the sample intake form in this book's appendix.)

My questionnaire asks potential clients about the theme colors of their wedding and asks them to describe in their own words what they want their painting to embody. I paint in an abstract impressionistic style for live events, so if I see someone describing their ideal painting as something photorealistic, I make it very clear that I do not paint in that style and to please review my work on my website to make sure they are comfortable with the look of what I will produce. Most of the time the clients realize they didn't really know what they wanted, just that they like your work, and so they decide to move forward. Others may realize your approach is not the right fit for them, which will save you from an unhappy client down the line.

As long as the client and I agree that my artistic style is what they would like to have, then I'm able to fine-tune my approach to what they want. They may want the work to embody certain colors or have a certain mood, or it may be crucial to them that certain people's likenesses are not left out of the finished product. One of my favorite questions to ask in my booking form is "describe your ideal wedding/event painting." This information, combined with the colors of the event and the those of the location where the artwork will eventually end up, makes it so that I am able to craft both the color and the composition that the client was envisioning.

The most basic way to make sure you are giving a client what they want in their painting is by determining what moment(s) they want to include in their painting and who they want to include. Make sure you discuss this in detail with your clients well before the event. I also include questions about these things in my booking form.

Challenges on the Scene

When I book an event, I always try to look up the venue online to see if I can locate images of its layout. I also ask clients if they can send me this, but it's something that often slips their mind. I really like to consider my composition as much as possible before I arrive at the scene of an event, but sometimes that kind of preparation just isn't possible. You have to remain flexible when it comes to composition and setup, or you'll give yourself too many headaches.

Sometimes you won't be located where you thought you would be. I can't tell you how many times I've had venue coordinators try to put me in a corner where nobody could see me. To avoid this I always ask the client to inform me and the venue ahead of time where they would like me to be. Sometimes this doesn't happen, though, and you will find yourself going toe to toe with a hotheaded, rushed coordinator. This is particularly common with weddings. When this happens, I invoke the name of the client (or the bride). I announce firmly that a huge part of the reason I was hired was because the client wants guests to be able to see me. I explain I am not just there to paint but also to perform, and I cannot perform if I am off in a hallway. Usually if you stand your ground and play a little bit of the artistic diva, suddenly a spot opens up for you. And while you can leverage the client's name in your negotiating, try not to get the client directly involved if you can avoid it—they usually have enough to occupy them while you are trying to set up, and they don't need added stress on their important day.

Similarly, I run into venue coordinators who don't want me to set up when I need to. They ask me to wait because they will be moving the furniture around or something along those lines. My timeline is very specific—I arrive when I need to and I need to start painting when I need to start painting. Again, if this happens to you, hold your ground. Especially if you are expected to deliver your painting by the end of the event, you will need all the time you can get. If they really give me trouble, I tell them I will set up and move when they need me to move. This is an inconvenience for me, but it is also a compromise when a coordinator won't cooperate.

Ugly Locations

Sometimes you arrive at an event location, and there is no denying it's ugly. Think musty 1970s lodge hall with paneled wood and fluorescent lights. You know this is not going to make a good painting. For such unfortunate cases, my advice for you is this: fudge it. You are a painter, after all, not a photographer. You have license to do what you need to do and tweak what you need to tweak to make sure your finished painting is both fantastic and what the client really wants. If you are more impressionistic or abstract like I am, this is not as difficult to pull off. It's common for me to add exciting layers of color to enhance a painting that may not have been present in real life. If you are a photorealist, keep to the principles of art and design. Stay true to the look of the room, but don't be afraid to use color combinations and your imagination in a way that will brighten things up, or you could omit some of the uglier room features all together. (Is the giant graying dead deer head an accessory the bride wants in the painting? Or is it something you can leave out?)

Lighting

Lighting, whether you are indoors or outdoors, is a huge issue when doing a live event painting. First, you need to make sure you have enough light, which is why you will have a light and require access to an electrical outlet for dark spaces. However, you also need to consider lighting that may change during the course of the event. If you are inside, the venue may have up-lighting that changes the room from the light-bulb yellow you see while you paint your ground to fluorescent pink or purple when the guests arrive. Ask the coordinator about colored up-lighting ahead of time if possible.

If you are outside, you need to consider the time of day. Are you painting at sunset? Does the client want a painting of the sunset, or do they want a painting that looks as though night has fallen because that is when the majority of the event will occur? Keep shifting shadows in mind also as the lighting changes.

Inclement Weather

Speaking of the outdoors, inclement weather can be a major issue. Even bright sunny days mean that you require protection from the sun. If it rains, a sturdy tent can fall short in protecting you and your gear if there is enough of a deluge. Even if you are painting inside, you will need to get all of your gear from your car to the venue, which can prove very difficult when it pours. You also don't want to look like a wet or sweaty mess as you're painting, so I suggest wearing comfortable clothing to set up and planning extra time to change into more appropriate event attire if possible. Sometimes I do wear my event outfit directly to the venue, but I never do my makeup until I am unloaded and set up in my spot.

Inclement weather can also be an issue that prevents you from arriving at the event at all. Depending on where you live and where your gigs are, snow, hurricanes, and the like may make it impossible for you to travel. In order to protect yourself, make sure to include in your contract what rights both you and the client have if you are unable to attend due to natural causes.

Illness

Your contract should also address what happens if you can't perform due to illness. In the early days of the COVID-19 pandemic, illness didn't just mean what would happen if I became sick—it had to cover the various changing scenarios of canceled and rescheduled events, or unsafe conditions due to high prevalence of COVID-19 in the community at the time of the event. I completely rewrote my contract for every event I booked moving forward from that time. The pandemic exposed holes in my contract that I had never seen before (mainly because I initially wrote it myself instead of hiring a lawyer), and the result was a major loss of income.

Gear Transportation

Sometimes transporting gear can create your largest hurdles. Be prepared for every scenario. I always bring an extra canvas with me to an event, because I fear that something will puncture the painting and I will have no backup. Make sure to store paints well for travel—exploding paint containers are more likely when everything is not well packed and being thrown around.

Traveling by air will introduce a completely different set of issues when it comes to getting your gear from point A to point B. I've spoken to many traveling artists, and here are some of the best tips I've gotten from them:

- **Canvas:** Have the canvas shipped to the hotel or venue ahead of time. Some artists will paint on multiple small canvas panels for events that require travel.

- **Paint:** Plan to check a bag with your paints if you are flying. You don't want to wrestle with the TSA over liquids rules. Make sure your paints are wrapped in multiple layers of plastic (see above regarding exploding paints) and make sure they are clearly labeled in the event that the TSA decides your paint tubes and brushes look like a bomb in the X-ray machine.

- **Easels:** If you paint small and use a plein air easel, air travel is not terrible. I recommend carrying your easel with you so it doesn't get damaged. If you prefer to check it, don't do so without putting it in a cushioned case. One artist I know paints large works of art on a huge easel and travels frequently by plane. She told me she had it custom made so that it could break down and fit into a special backpack she could carry.

- **Finished art:** If you are an artist who takes your work home to finish in the studio, long-distance travel may not be for you. It is best to be able to leave a painting with the client at the end of the event when traveling so you don't have the liability of trying to bring it back home in one piece. If you truly need to send it home, I highly recommend arranging for shipping or a private courier. Be sure to keep this in mind when you price your art, as shipping can be expensive.

Damages

What if your painting does get damaged and you have only one canvas? It sounds like a nightmare scenario, right? There isn't too much you can do, unfortunately, but you'll need to take a deep breath. Keep going! Finish the painting as well as you can. If you can tape up a tear or hole from the back of the canvas, do it. However, you will need to either fully repair the canvas, if possible, or repaint the painting on a new canvas after the event. Since that's the last thing you want to have to do, I always bring a spare canvas.

Another nightmare scenario you will want to avoid is paint spills. You absolutely do not want to damage a location if you can help it. This is why I set up a layer of plastic drop cloth and canvas drop cloth with a wide berth around me. Sometimes, a little paint still escapes somehow. If it's a small spill, it's likely it won't even be noticed by the venue as stains from food and drinks are common. However, if it's obvious you've made a mess, come clean to the venue after the event is over. See what you can work out to make things right—worst-case scenario, you have liability insurance for a reason.

Misbehaving Guests

As I've noted, guests love to come talk to you while you paint. You will need to be okay with this, as your ability to interact with your audience will be part of your appeal. However, some lines need not be crossed. I can't tell you how many times I've had guests get a little too close and even touch me inappropriately. While it's easy to want to ignore such behavior for the sake of the event, make sure you are professional and set your boundaries. If a guest behaves really poorly, ask for help from the venue staff instead of trying to involve your clients.

Drunk guests and art supplies do not mix. It's awful when people back up against you while you paint, and you certainly don't want anyone to trip on any wires or easel legs. This is when roping off your painting area can be a real benefit. A physical barrier that is not too imposing will make it possible for you to talk to guests but still maintain a safe distance.

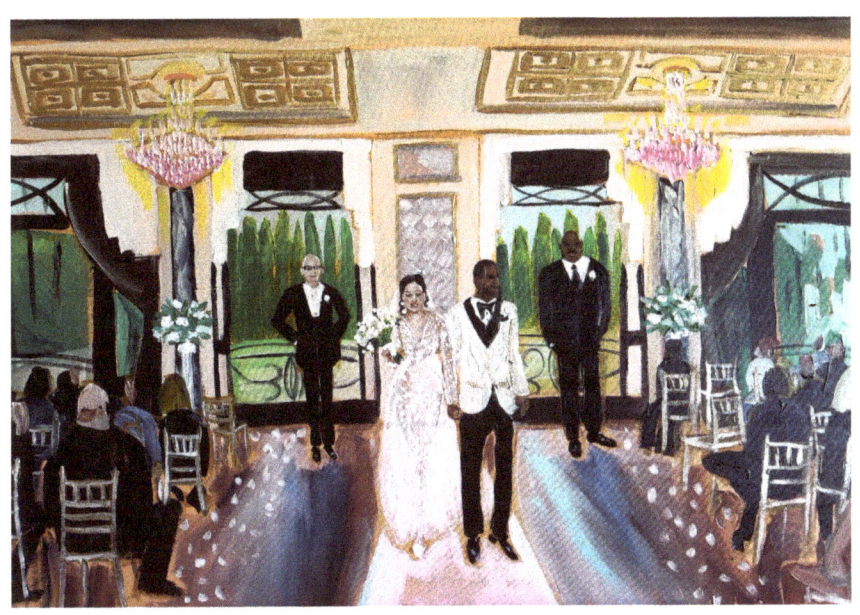

17

AND IN THE END...

In writing this book, some of my circle of friends wondered at my desire to share my secrets with other artists and literally create my own competition. My reasoning for doing this is that artists are too often overlooked and abused. We struggle in many ways, and while other artists are the only ones who can truly understand our struggle, they are often not in a position to help us.

Writing a book that helps other artists convert their practice to something that makes them money is one thing that I can do to help. I believe in karma—what goes around comes around. Many people have helped me in different ways in my lifetime, and I want to make a difference for others however I can.

Learning to live paint from a book is a wonderful place to start, because artists need access to basic information on how to run a business and this book communicates that start-up information well. However, so much of the job is learned in the practice. That's why my work teaching artists to be live event painters doesn't stop here.

I have a Facebook group membership available for Live Painters to ask for help with specific barriers they encounter to offer overflow gig opportunities (when I get an inquiry for a date when I am already booked, I refer the client to my students for live painting event coverage). Go to Facebook and search "The Live Painter's Guidebook Group" to join, or follow the direct link: https://www.facebook.com/thelivepainter.

I also offer comprehensive classes on the live painting process and individual coaching for new live event artists. I help my students troubleshoot creative and business problems, help them improve their paintings, and let them work with me at real events. I offer private event coaching at my students' live events to help them through the inevitable, unpredictable challenges they will come across that only exist in real-life scenarios. If you have found this book inspiring and useful, and are serious about starting your business as a Live Painter, consider the investment of one-to-one sessions and how much it will help you grow your business in the long term. After all, you would be working *with* the Live Painter. Not only am I happy to help you, but you'll have fun working with me, and you will be making a business investment with a high return rate—you will very quickly make more money live painting your events than the cost of training.

This really is the coolest paying job an artist can find! What other job exists where you get paid to paint (and paid well, I might add) while attending parties? I'm so happy you've discovered it. Now go out there, and let the world discover your art!

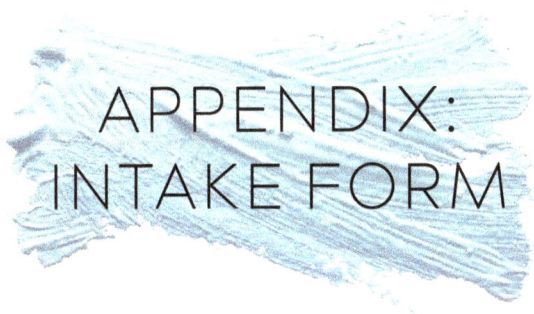

APPENDIX: INTAKE FORM

Create an intake form or questionnaire to gather all the information you need to draw up a contract and deliver the client the product they have in mind.

Intake Form for Live Wedding Paintings

1. **Today's Date**
2. **Basic Info**
   - Your name
   - Email
   - Address
   - Phone number
   - Name of two people getting married
   - Their address if different from yours
   - What is your relationship to the wedding couple?
   - One month prior to the wedding, I will reach out to the main contact to confirm the details in this questionnaire and review for any changes. Who should I call?
   - How did you hear about us?
3. **About the Wedding**
   - Wedding date

- What is the exact address of where the live painting will take place?
- Ceremony start time
- Cocktail hour start time
- Reception start time
- Reception end time
- Is the ceremony, cocktail hour, or reception located in the same room? This helps me calculate arrival time needed.
- If needed, please explain the setup of the wedding location further.
- What is the theme/vibe/feel of your wedding?
- What are your wedding colors, if known?

4. **About the Painting**
   - Is this painting a gift or surprise?
   - What part of the wedding do you want painted?
   - Besides the wedding couple, is there anybody specific who should be depicted in the painting? (The maximum number depends on canvas size; please list people in order of priority.)
   - Is there a specific moment you would like to include in the painting? (The most popular moment is the first dance, but I can work out almost any vision you have.)
   - Write up to three words you would use to describe your ideal finished painting.
   - What is your preferred canvas size?
   - If a custom size is desired, please indicate your preference here (I will confirm if this size is available and provide the pricing).
   - Any other special requests or information you want me to know for your painting?

5. **Venue/Location Details**
   - Earliest access time for vendors for painting location?
   - Describe the parking. Anything I may need to know for carrying heavy equipment alone is important!
   - Are stairs required to access the painting location?
   - Is there access to an electrical outlet? (Required for dark locations.)
   - Is there access to running water?

- Is there shelter from sun/rain to paint under if outdoors? (Required if outdoors.)
- Is there at least a 10-by-10-foot space for the artist?
- Name and contact info for any wedding planner/day-of coordinator/reception coordinator
- Does your venue require liability insurance from vendors?
- Is there anything else I should know about your venue/painting location?

5. **Day-of Details**
   - Will a meal be provided to the Live Painter at the event?
   - Most paintings are finished by the end of the event and are mostly if not completely dry. Please choose your painting transportation: will you or a designated family/friend be taking the painting home OR would you like the artist to transport it to the studio and arrange for pick up/delivery later?
- In the event your painting is not finished, I will finish it in my studio. How would you like to retrieve it?

Intake Form for Live Event Paintings (Non-Wedding)

1. **Today's Date**
2. **Basic Info**
   - Your name
   - Email
   - Address
   - Phone number
   - What kind of event is this? If there is a guest of honor please include their name.
   - Their address if different from yours
   - What is your relationship to the event?
   - One month prior to the event, I will reach out to the main contact to confirm the details in this questionnaire and review for any changes. Who should I call?

 • How did you hear about us?

3. **About the Event**

 • Event date
 • What is the exact address of where the live painting will take place?
 • Event start time
 • Event end time
 • If needed, please explain the setup of the event location further.
 • What is the theme/vibe/feel of your event?
 • What are your event colors, if known?

4. **About the Painting**

 • Is this painting a gift or surprise?
 • Is there anybody specific who should be depicted in the painting? (Maximum number depends on canvas size; please list people in order of priority.)
 • Is there a specific moment you would like to include in the painting?
 • Write up to three words you would use to describe your ideal finished painting.
 • What is your preferred canvas size?
 • If custom size is desired, please indicate preference here (I will confirm if this size is available and provide the pricing).
 • Any other special requests or information you want me to know for your painting?

5. **Venue/Location Details**

 • Earliest access time for vendors for painting location?
 • Describe the parking. Anything I may need to know for carrying heavy equipment alone is important!
 • Are stairs required to access the painting location?
 • Is there access to an electrical outlet? (Required for dark locations.)
 • Is there access to running water?
 • Is there shelter from sun/rain to paint under if outdoors? (Required if outdoors.)
 • Is there at least a 10-by-10-foot space for the artist?

- Name and contact info for any wedding planner/day-of coordinator/reception coordinator
- Does your venue require liability insurance from vendors?
- Is there anything else I should know about your venue/painting location?

6. **Day-of Details**
   - Will a meal be provided to the Live Painter at the event?
   - Most paintings are finished by the end of the event and are mostly if not completely dry. Please choose your painting transportation: will you or a designated family/friend be taking the painting home OR would you like the artist to transport it to the studio and arrange for pick up/delivery later?
   - In the event your painting is not finished, I will finish it in my studio. How would you like to retrieve it?

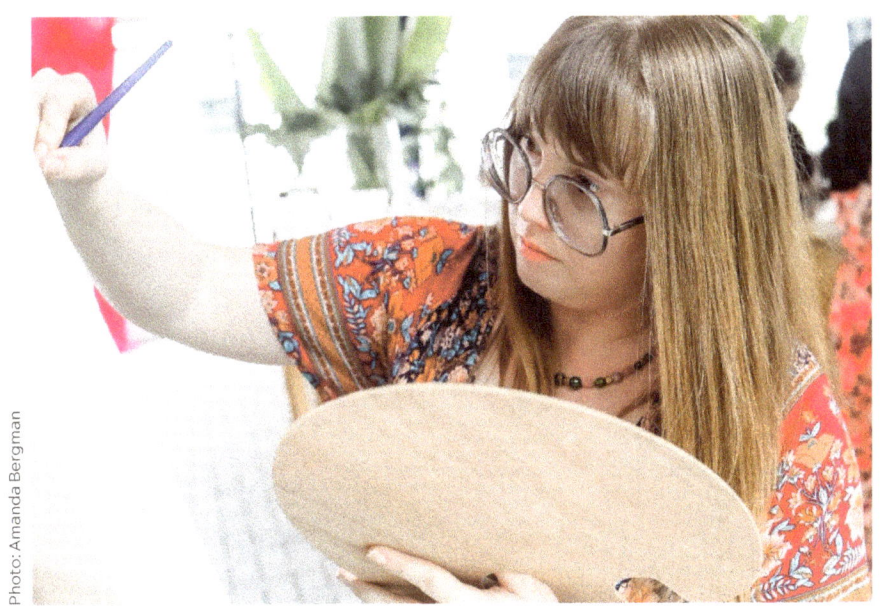

ABOUT THE AUTHOR

Lauryn Ahearn was born in North Carolina, but has spent most of her life growing up in New Jersey, where she currently resides. Art has always been an integral part of life for her—she has been painting and drawing for as long as she can remember. She studied Visual Arts and graduated with a B.F.A. from the competitive Mason Gross School of the Arts at Rutgers University in 2005. She has exhibited in galleries in New York City and New Jersey.

Lauryn is proud to share the skills she has developed through two decades of professional art making with her wonderful clients. Her pleasant, always cheery demeanor, bolstered by several years of experience as a professional actress and improviser, draws viewers to her live performances. Onlookers are swept up into the journey of the artwork, as they watch layers of paint build, melt, and glaze into a dreamy reflection of their surroundings.

Lauryn's heartfelt connection to intimate and unseen moments and feelings of her subjects is at the core of her live painting. She captures cherished moments in her clients' lives that will transport them back to their special moment in a way that photos and videos can's match.

Lauryn works primarily in New York City, Philadelphia, New Jersey, and the surrounding areas. However, she will travel to any location for any event.

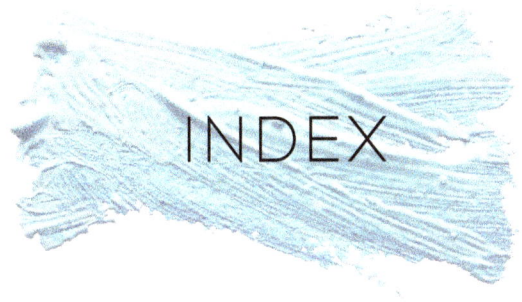

INDEX

www.ingramcontent.com/pod-product-compliance
Lightning Source LLC
Chambersburg PA
CBHW042133280526

45792CB00018B/2331